The Gun Digest Book of

Gun Care Cleaning & Refinishing

Book One: Handguns

by J. B. Wood

DBI Books, Inc., Northfield, Ill.

About Our Covers

In case you hadn't noticed, the "Good Old Boys" at Omark/CCI added Outer Labs to their growing family of products for shooters.

As we all know, Outers has a long-standing, superb reputation with shooters and hunters worldwide. We are indeed proud to have Outers' products featured on the outside covers of this the *Gun Digest Book of Gun Care Cleaning & Refinishing, Book One: Handguns*.

In the center of the cover you'll see one of Outers latest offerings. It's their new Silverline handgun case made of tough aluminum and featuring egg-carton type foam lining for maximum firearms protection; the case is, of course, lockable for security.

Surrounding the new Silverline case is a full selection of Outers gun care and maintenance products. They include the Outers Gun Blue Kit, the Short Barrel Pistol Cleaning Kit and the new (and beautifully made) "Imperial" Rifle/Pistol Cleaning Rod. You'll also see Outers new line of aerosol gun care products—Crud Cutter™ (degreaser), Nitro Solvent, Water Shed™ (silicone water and stain repellent) and Tri-Lube™, a superb Teflon® based lubricant, cleaner and rust inhibitor.

Our inside covers feature one of the oldest gun-care equipment outfits in the U.S., RIG Products Company. For almost a half century RIG has provided shooters with their famous Rust Inhibiting Grease ("RIG Universal"). It's designed to fully protect a firearm from the elements of foul weather, or serve as long term protection during storage.

Seen on our inside front cover is, of course, a jar of RIG Universal grease, followed by some of the newer members of the RIG family of gun-care products, including: RIG 3, a superb degreaser, RIG 2, a light-oil lubricant and a jar of RIG +P Stainless Steel Lube (a sample of which is included with every Randall Stainless Steel auto that leaves the factory).

Also pictured are RIG's Universal grease, a sheepskin RIG-Rag and the new, custom-quality RIG-Rod for handguns, complete with jags, brushes and loop tips.

On our inside back cover you'll see a jar and tube of the traditional RIG Universal grease as well as a jar each of RIG +P Stainless Steel Lube and RIG Black Powder Patch Lube. Also present is an aerosol can of RIG 3, a superb degreaser, and an aerosol can of RIG 2 Oil Lubricant.

In the center are some of RIG's newest offerings. They include a bronze action brush, RIG-Rod for rifles, along with bronze brushes and loop-tips in various calibers. The bronze action brush as well as the RIG-Rod and accessories are all resting on the traditional sheepskin RIG-Rag. Photos by John Hanusin.

About the Author

Guns, especially automatic pistols, have always been a part of J.B. Wood's life, and it has now been almost 35 years since he began working as a gunsmith. Fortunately, Wood has been able to combine his mechanical talents with writing about them, which he's been doing since 1962. In that time he has had more than 400 articles published in *Gun Digest, Guns Illustrated* and in most of the monthly gun magazines. In 1977-1978 he authored a two-book series for DBI Books, *Troubleshooting Your Handgun* and *Troubleshooting Your Rifle and Shotgun*. From 1979 to 1981, Wood wrote and photographed the six-part *Firearms Assembly/Disassembly* series, a monumental task that turned out to be the best reference ever printed on the subject at hand.

In 1974, J.B. Wood began a regular monthly relationship with gun magazines. He was Gunsmithing Editor for *Guns & Ammo* magazine for eight years, is Contributing Editor to *Gun Digest* and *Combat Handguns*, and currently is Gunsmithing Editor for *Shooting Times* magazine. Because he is so well briefed on firearms in general, and self-loading pistols in particluar, Wood is considered to an international authority, and has testified in many court cases involving firearms as an expert witness. In addition, he has done mechanical design and redesign work for a number of domestic and foreign arms makers. Currently he is a full-time gunsmith, writer, and firearms consultant and lives in rural Kentucky.

ISBN 0-910676-78-x

The views and opinions of the author expressed herein are not necessarily those of the publisher, and no responsiblity for such views will be assumed.

Arms and Armour Press, London, G.B., exclusive licencees and distributors in Britain and Europe; Australaiasia, Nigeria, South Africa and Zimbabwe; India and Pakistan; Singapore, Hong Kong and Japan.

Library of Congress Catalog Card #84-071764

Table of Contents

Acknowledgements

My thanks to these people, who helped to make this book possible: Doug Wright, Al Selleck, Charles Magee, Arnold Carlson, Bill Cooper, Jim Brobst, Doug Evans, Lee Keppler, Milt Settar, Brady Brown, Richard Simons, John Stupero, Anthony Rupp, Ted Freeland, Dave Ecker, Larry Ference, John Bressem, Larry Larsen, Al Skaar, Bob and Frank Brownell, Ted Bottomley, Richard Floyd, J. A. Lane, Glenn Blackshaw, Bill Wilson, Jim Kelley, George Miska, Darrell Reed, Pauline McIntosh, Bruce Jennings, George Jennings, Paul M. Fulkerson, Dave Manson, Alexander Zemke, James Mongello, Robert Greenberg, Robert Ellsworth, Michael Kera, Wayne Gurowsky, Ed House, Gary Geier.

A special thanks to Michael Schmidt, for expert developing and printing of my photos.

Introduction

AFTER 10 YEARS of answering firearms questions as "The Gunsmith" in two monthly magazines, there are certain questions that I know will be in each month's mail from readers. The most frequent will be "How much is it worth?", "Where can I find parts?", and "How can I take it apart?"—in that order.

I specifically avoid trying to answer the value questions, since only a hands-on appraisal can give an accurate figure. The parts questions are easier. I can either send the inquirer to a known source, or tell him to look for a good gunsmith and have the parts made. As for the takedown questions, DBI Books and this writer have produced a six-volume answer to most of those.

There are other Gunsmith-column questions, though, that are difficult to cover thoroughly in the necessarily brief monthly column format. For example, is it harmful to an automatic pistol magazine to leave it fully loaded for long periods of time? The correct answer to this one varies, and depends on several factors. This question would fall into the "Gun Care" category.

Here's one that's even more complicated: The old hands say that cleaning direction should always be from the breech toward the muzzle. However, modern solid-frame revolvers and most muzzle-loaders can't be cleaned that way. Does cleaning from front-to-rear harm the rifling at the muzzle? Obviously, a "Cleaning" question, and one that requires more than a one-paragraph answer.

Another subject that often appears in the mailbag is refinishing. Several years ago, in *Guns Illustrated*, I wrote two articles which gave a general view of the then-offered finishes, but both were mostly a "here's what's available" presentation. What is the toughest finish, and which is best in a particular use? Also, since then, several new finishes have been developed, such as Electroless Nickel and Lubri-Bond.

So, DBI Books, Inc. and this writer decided to put together a complete treatment of the three questions mentioned: **Care, Cleaning,** and **Refinishing**—and you have one-half of this effort in your hands (the other volume covers rifles and shotguns). One added note on the refinishing section: It's *not* a how-to-do-it treatise on the subject, but rather a how-to-choose-wisely discussion.

J. B. Wood
Raintree House
Corydon, Kentucky

Section One

Gun Care

WHEN I FIRST thought of writing this portion of the book, I intended to cover mainly mechanical questions, such as the long-loaded magazine, dry-firing, and so on. After some further thought, though, it occurred to me that "care" has a much more extensive scope. It includes mechanical questions, of course, but it should also include safety in handling, security and storage, and several other aspects of firearms care. On some of these points, my observations may seem rather obvious to experienced gun people, but I'm assuming that some who read this book may be beginners. You "old hands" can just skim over the parts that strike you as being too elementary.

Dry-Firing

First, let's look at some of the mechanical considerations, and begin with one of the most-asked questions: Is dry-firing harmful to the internal parts of a handgun? A quick and general answer would be "Sometimes," but it's not that simple.

Serious shooters often keep a target on the wall of the den, office, or gunroom, and practice sight alignment and trigger squeeze with an empty handgun. Over the years, this can add up to a lot of "snaps," and many will say that this practice has never damaged their guns. On the other hand, there are numerous cases in which damage can be traced directly to dry-firing. This frequently depends on the particular gun involved. Some are more tolerant of this than others.

It might be well to consider for a moment the possible effect of dry-firing on a very important part, the firing pin. When a handgun is fired

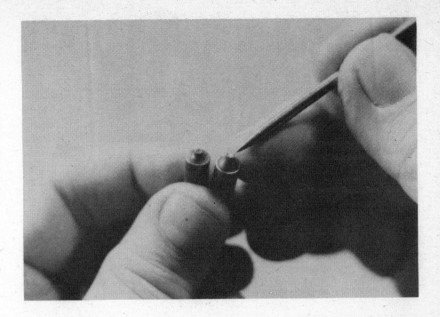

Two broken strikers, from true hammerless automatics. It's probably not visible in the photo, but the broken firing pin tips show the sparkle of crystallization.

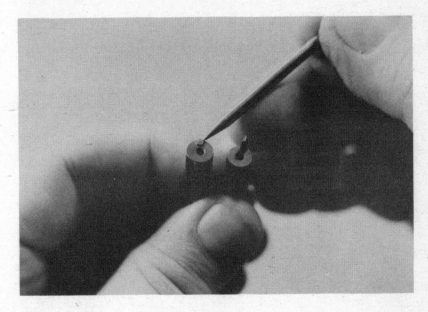

A broken striker from a 22 automatic pistol, shown with a new replacement. Offset firing pins of this type seem to be particularly prone to breakage.

with a cartridge in the chamber, the impact of the firing pin point is somewhat cushioned as it encounters the relatively soft metal of the cartridge primer. This principle is applied in the snap-caps that were once supplied as accessories with fine English shotguns. In those, a dummy shell had the primer replaced with a resilient material or a spring-loaded plug to soften the end of the firing pin's forward movement.

In dry-firing, the firing pin comes to a very sudden and abrupt stop. I'm not a metallurgist, but a person well-versed in that arcane knowledge once described the effect to me this way: When a small piece of steel, such as a firing pin point, is in motion and is suddenly stopped, some of the inner molecular structure continues to drift in the direction of the original motion. As the action is repeated, the density of the point is increased, and it becomes brittle. I'm not sure that all of my terminology is correct,

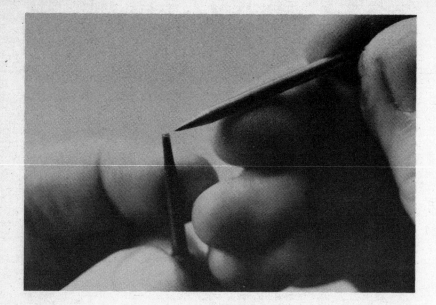

This firing pin, from an external-hammer automatic, fractured only at its extreme tip, and was causing only occasional misfires. An inertia type, it still had enough reach to work part of the time.

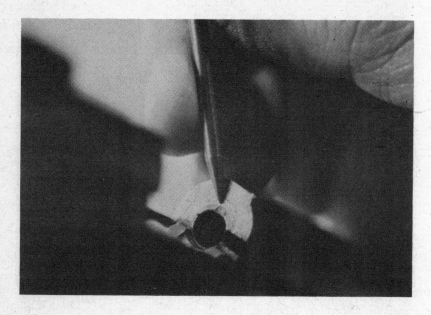

A typical chamber-edge dent in a pistol chambered for 22 Long Rifle. The pistol had been extensively dry-fired.

and I'm putting this down as I understood it, but it does sound logical.

And, it would explain a lot of broken firing pins. If the firing pin were tempered extra-hard by the factory, that would make it happen sooner. A few years ago, one small batch of otherwise excellent Star automatic pistols slipped past the final inspection in Eibar with very hard firing pins, and by chance I got two of them. Shortly after I traded for the pistols, my 9mm Star BKM and 22 Star FM both had broken firing pin points. I made replacements from semi-hardened drill rod, and have been shooting both pistols for around 10 years, with no further problems.

Another factor to be considered is the mass of the firing pin, and the distance it moves. The effect would be lessened, for example, in the small, short, in-the-frame firing pin of a modern revolver. In comparison, there is frequent break-

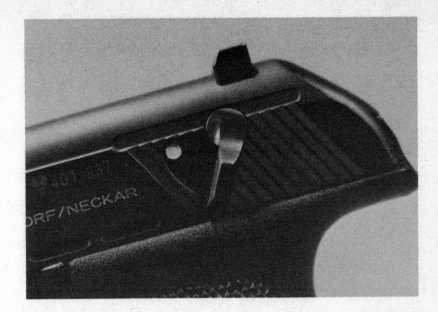

The Heckler & Koch P9S and the Star Model 28 have firing pin block safety systems that do not disconnect the trigger linkage. With the safety in on-safe position, they can be dry-fired without harm.

age in the long-traveling strikers of the true hammerless automatics. It's also interesting to note that firing pin material other than steel has occasionally been used, with some success. Some of the early Colt 38 automatics had bronze firing pins, and I've never seen a broken one. In more recent times, the beryllium-copper alloy firing pin of the Charter Arms revolver has proved to be virtually unbreakable.

It has been reasoned by some that in external-hammer handguns that have a firing pin return spring, the spring will cushion the end-stop of the firing pin, and prevent damage. In auto pistols such as the Colt Government Model and the Browning Hi-Power, which have rather strong return springs, this may have some validity. In most handguns, though, the return spring is very light, and has very little dampening effect.

The 22 rimfire is, of course, another case. (An unintentional pun, but I think I'll leave it.)

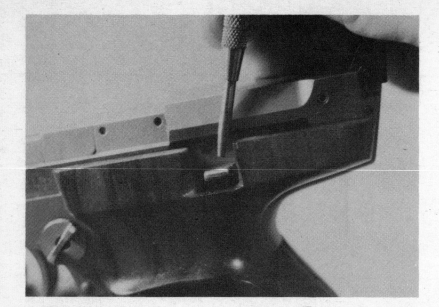

The fine Danish Agner Model 80, a true target pistol, has a dry-firing device. Shown in the cocked mode, the pedal will fly upward when the trigger is depressed. The device gives exactly the same trigger pull feel as in actual sear release.

From long wear, the firing pin aperture in the breech face of this British Webley revolver has lost its round shape, but there is no protrusion. When the edges of the aperture do become extruded, this can cause cylinder rotation difficulties.

Even non-serious shooters are usually aware that snapping a rimfire on an empty chamber is a bad idea. Some handguns, such as the early Hi-Standard autos, have firing pins designed to stop before the point touches the rear face of the barrel. Many guns, though, have unlimited travel, and when the firing pin point repeatedly strikes the barrel at the chamber edge, a dent will begin to form which will eventually interfere with loading and extraction. Or, the firing pin point will

break. Usually, both will happen.

On some serious 22 target pistols—my beautiful Agner from Denmark is an example—there is a mechanical provision for dry-firing practice. With the hammer at rest, uncocked, a sear-lever can be depressed, and it is released by a normal trigger pull. This device gives exactly the same "feel" as actually dropping the hammer, and allows unlimited practice without any stressing of the firing system parts. If your 22

Simple snap caps can be made by removing the primers from fired cartridge cases, and replacing them with pads of nylon, rubber, or hard leather. Using an adjustable leather punch, the one shown was made in about 3 minutes. Urethane cement was used to secure the leather pad in the primer pocket.

rimfire handgun doesn't have something like this, though, don't snap it when empty!

Aside from possible breakage of the firing pin point, there is another area of damage that can occur in some handguns, especially in revolvers having a short firing pin with minimal point extension. Repeated impact of the shoulder behind the point against the inner shoulder of the firing pin tunnel can eventually upset the breech face around the firing pin aperture, forcing it out-

ward. If this becomes very pronounced, it can cause the cartridge case heads to bind, preventing cylinder rotation. A variation of this condition can occur in revolvers which have a hammer-mounted firing pin which tilts—the underside of the tip first striking the bottom of the aperture. In this case, the lower edge of the aperture can be extruded outward, with similar results.

This situation can also occur in automatic pistols, when the firing pin point is short and the breech face is relatively thin. In all cases, revolver or auto, the occurrence of this syndrome can depend on several factors, and the heat-treatment of the parts involved is more significant than the design of the parts. Even when the firing pin point is short and the breech face is thin, proper hardening of the breech face can prevent any outward peening from happening. Unfortunately, most firing pins are harder than the breech face, so this is a factor to consider if you choose to dry-fire.

There is another type of dry-firing damage that can occur in certain low-priced handguns that have slides or frames made of non-ferrous alloys. In these guns, in dry-firing, the steel hammer has unimpeded impact on the rear inner face of the alloy slide or frame. Extensive dry-firing can upset the area around the firing pin head, sometimes to an extent that the firing pin will be jammed. When this occurs, the amateur gunsmith will frequently chamfer the rear edges of the firing pin tunnel, thereby reducing the impact area even more. This will allow the hammer, in full-down position, to tip forward beyond its normal resting point. If the firing pin was originally an inertia-type, this property has

now been effectively canceled. The only proper way to repair this situation, after peening has occurred, would be to install a steel collar in the slide to surround the firing pin head.

Better still, to prevent the damage, just don't snap an alloy handgun when it's empty. Unlike some of my fellow-writers, I have never had the opinion that the low-priced alloy guns were "bad." While they don't have the long-term durability of finer guns, they afford a measure of protection to people of limited means. Any gun which equalizes the situation between a little old lady in a housing project and three young thugs who are breaking in her door is a good gun.

The snap caps mentioned earlier are available commercially in a few of the most popular handgun calibers, but I have often made my own. For dry-firing, or for dropping an internal hammer or the striker of a true hammerless gun, they are nice to have. And, they are not difficult to make. Just take an empty, un-primed case in any caliber, and make a plug of nylon or dense rubber (motor mount rubber is excellent), fitting it tightly into the primer pocket of the case. Trim it off level with the case head, and you have a snap-cap that will cushion the firing pin point for many dry-firings.

Mainspring Tension

In automatic pistols, some of the so-called hammerless guns actually have a pivoting hammer inside, hidden by the slide. Others are true hammerless guns, having a striker that travels in a tunnel within the slide, with the front of the striker reduced to become the firing pin. With either system, internal hammer or striker, the gun is cocked each time the slide is cycled. This presents a dilemma for owners of these guns who are concerned about care: Which is worse —leaving the gun cocked during storage, or dropping the hammer or striker on an empty chamber?

This is another of those questions that shouldn't be given a general answer. Individual guns can have differences in mainspring quality, even in guns from the same manufacturer. A few pistols, such as the Colt Model M, the Czech P-27, and the Russian Makarov, have blade-type mainsprings, and these are less likely to lose tension from long compression. On the other hand, these "flat" springs tend to be somewhat more prone to breakage. Nearly all modern autos have helical-coil hammer springs or striker springs. These rarely break, but if their tempering was not carefully done, long-term compression can sometimes cause them to "take a set" and lose tension.

The result of this, obviously, would be misfires, since the hammer or striker would not deliver enough firing pin impact to detonate the cartridge primer. If the gun is being used as a police back-up piece or for civilian personal protection, a misfiring incident could have a very serious effect. My answer to the question is that in most cases, leaving the gun cocked will probably do no harm. Where personal protection is involved, though, that "probably" bothers me. Speaking for myself, I always pull the trigger and drop the hammer. If I have a snap-cap cartridge in the caliber involved, I use it. If not, well, an occasional hammer or striker drop is not the same as endless dry-firing practice. When the pistol is a 22 rimfire, I insert an empty 22 cartridge case, with its head turned so the firing pin point will strike an area away from the original firing pin indentation. This will give the same cushioning effect as when a live round is fired.

To sum up the mainspring question, some springs can be left compressed for long periods and will go on working forever. Others will take a set, and will eventually have to be replaced. Unfortunately, there is no way to be certain whether any particular spring will be affected. So, I'd advise letting the hammer drop, just to be sure.

A thought just occurred to me—what about the external hammer pistols that are carried extensively in the "cocked-and-locked" mode? Well, the same possibility of eventual tension loss exists for them. When the gun is the Colt Government Model or one of its copies, though, there is so much extra allowance in hammer spring strength that if there is some weakening, it will probably cause no problem.

Magazines

While we're on the subject of springs that may lose tension if compressed over long periods of time, let's deal with one of the most-asked auto pistol questions: Is it harmful to leave a magazine fully loaded for weeks, months, or even years? Those who use an automatic only for recreational or match target shooting may find the question ridiculous—their pistols are fully loaded only during shooting sessions, and are stored empty.

For many, though, this is not the case. Those who use an auto pistol for personal or home defense, and those in law enforcement who carry automatics, are likely to keep them fully loaded at all times. In this usage, the possibility of a weakened magazine spring that could affect feeding is a very understandable concern. So, is there a chance that leaving a magazine fully loaded, day in and day out, will possibly damage the spring? I used to think so. Quite a few years ago, when I first began using automatics extensively, I even followed the practice of loading my "carrying" magazines short by one round—or, if the gun were a large-capacity type, such as the Browning HP, by two rounds. My reasoning was that if the spring was not fully compressed, it wouldn't be likely to take a set and weaken. Two separate incidents taught me that I needn't have bothered.

The first involved an acquaintance who had discovered, among his late father's attic-stored possessions, a fully-loaded U.S. Army issue Colt Government Model pistol. It was the true 1911 model, and by questioning other family members he established that the gun had been placed in storage prior to 1920. At the time he brought it to me for testing and evaluation, it had been loaded for more than 50 years! I didn't fire the World War One ammo that was in the gun—I gave the cartridges to the owner to keep.

Those who carry an automatic pistol as part of their work frequently keep magazines loaded for long periods of time. Whether this can cause deterioration of the magazine spring is an open question. Much depends on the quality and design of the individual pistol and its springs.

An amateur attempt at adjustment of the feed lips of this hard-tempered Radom magazine resulted in breakage of both sides of the magazine at the top. It is possible to rework damaged magazines, but it's a job for a professional, and some magazines must be pre-annealed.

I did, though, load the fine old piece with fresh 45 caliber rounds, and fired three full magazines. It functioned perfectly.

The other incident involved my own venerable Browning Hi-Power, made in October of 1943, when Nazi troops were strutting in Herstal. As originally made, the double-column magazine held 13 rounds. Over the years, I acquired several spare magazines, and I noticed that some of them easily held 14 rounds. Disas-

sembly of the magazines showed that the ones holding an extra round differed only in the length of the spring-lug on the underside of the follower. One other thing was also revealed: When the magazines were fully loaded, the spring was not completely compressed.

Subsequently, I checked the magazines of other automatic pistols, and found that while there were a few exceptions, this "extra spring space" was a usual thing. When I discovered this, I stopped "short-loading" my magazines. For those who may still worry about it, there's an easy solution: Obtain an extra magazine, and carry one while leaving the other unloaded, to rest the spring. Switch them every month or so. This will probably make the chronic worrier feel better about it, but I don't believe it's necessary.

Aside from the spring question, there are other types of magazine damage that can occur. Even though they are made of relatively thin sheet steel, most magazines are remarkably sturdy. Still, it's possible to dent the body or deform the feed lips, especially if the magazine is dropped on hard and uneven surfaces while fully loaded. The extra weight of the cartridges will add to the impact force.

Another damage possibility is present when the magazine is slammed into its well with force. The floorplate extension will tend to stop it short of impacting against the underside of the breechblock at the top, but often there is enough vertical play that the feed lips can touch. Even a very slight deformation of one or both of the feed lips can cause the cartridges to jam as they are picked up by the breech face of the slide. Prevention of this sort of thing is elementary— push the magazine gently and firmly into place until it is caught by the catch. Never slam it.

If damage has occurred in spite of precautions, or if a previous owner has abused a magazine, don't try to adjust the feed lips with pliers. When this is attempted, the magazine is usually ruined, beyond repair. Consult a gunsmith, and take his advice on whether the magazine is repairable, or should be replaced. The magazine is the least expensive major part of an automatic pistol, and the cost of one is a low price to pay for reliable operation.

When an automatic pistol misfeeds, don't be too quick to blame the magazine. There are several other factors involved in feeding, the principal ones being the feed ramp and the extractor. In locked-breech autos that have a moving barrel, the changing barrel position is a factor. Bullet shape and type are also significant. On any of these points, consult a gunsmith.

Extractors and Ejectors

The terminology sometimes gets a little mixed, and the two items above are not the same when applied to automatics and revolvers. I'll try defining them, but this may just add to the confusion. Strictly speaking, an extractor is located to the rear of the chamber, and *pulls* the cartridge case out. An ejector is located beside or below the chamber, and *pushes* the case out. So far, so good, when the terms are applied separately to automatics and revolvers.

An automatic, however, will usually have both an extractor and an ejector, and in this case the latter term refers to a part that is normally fixed in place. Its function, after the extractor has pulled the fired cartridge case from the chamber, is to kick the case out the ejection port. The auto pistol ejector is usually a sturdy part, not prone to breakage, and it requires no special care.

In many pistols, the same minimum care advice can be applied to extractors, but there are exceptions. In some automatics, the bevel of the extractor beak is a very shallow angle. With these, the extractor engages the rim of the cartridge case easily if the cartridge is being fed from the magazine, but it's not as tolerant of a round dropped into the chamber, single-loaded. The beak of the extractor will usually climb the cartridge rim and snap over it, but the steep angle imparts a severe mechanical strain. In pistols having extractors with this shape, I've seen several cases of breakage when a single round was dropped into the chamber and the slide was allowed to snap shut on it. So, know your gun. If

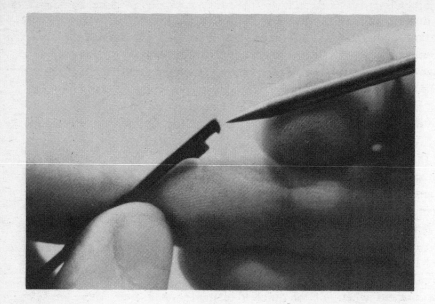

Some extractors, having rather blunt front surfaces on the beak, are intolerant of single rounds dropped into the chamber of the pistol.

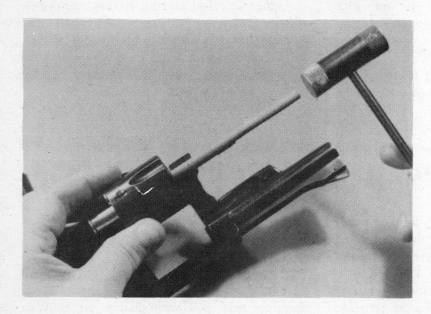

To remove stuck cases from a revolver, use a wood or nylon dowel and a small hammer to tap them out, as shown. If the cases are stuck very tightly, the edge of the cylinder should be rested on the edge of a non-marring surface for this operation.

it has a steep extractor beak, don't single-load it. Feed all cartridges from the magazine. Even if the pistol has a sharp extractor beak angle, and is tolerant of single-loading, this is a good idea. The system was designed to work that way.

Some revolver manufacturers persist in referring to the star-shaped extensions of the cylinder ratchet as an "extractor." Since it pushes the cartridge cases out rather than pulling them, I'll agree with Colt and Ruger and call it an ejector. Since revolver loading is manual, there are no problems on the way into the chambers. A certain combination of factors, though, can result in problems on the way out: These can be tool marks or other roughness in the chambers, lead accumulation, a poorly-fitted ejector, tired brass that fails to rebound after obturation, or any combination of the above. When one or more of these things occur, a push on the ejector rod after firing will meet firm resistance. In this situation, a shooter's reaction will often be to strike the end of the ejector rod with some non-marring object, or bump the end of the rod against something, such as the edge of a range bench. Both are bad moves.

With cases firmly stuck in the chambers, impact on the ejector rod can cause damage in several ways. The most obvious would be that the rod may be bent or broken. Quite often not all of the cases are stuck, and this will put an uneven strain on the ejector star. If so, it's possible that one arm of the ejector may be broken or deformed. With enough force applied, the cylinder crane could be sprung.

The right way to deal with stuck cases is to keep in your range box a short length of wood or nylon dowel, and a small hammer. Resting one edge of the cylinder on the shooting bench to avoid crane damage, insert the dowel rod into each chamber from the front, and use the hammer to gently tap out the cases, one at a time. If the problem occurs with some regularity, consult a gunsmith and take corrective measures.

Cylinder Latches, Timing

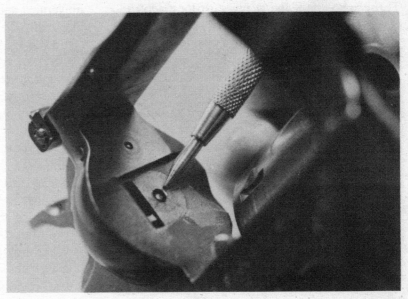

The tool is pointing to the cylinder locking pin hole in the breech face. Repeated slamming of the cylinder can eventually cause deformation of its wall, and a bulge into the cylinder hand slot.

There is one element in revolver handling that is in the same category as slamming the magazine into an automatic. Anyone who watches even a minimum of movies or television will eventually see some character in the story check the loads in his revolver, then flick the cylinder back into place with a snap of his wrist. I'm always pleased when it's the bad guy who does this—perhaps his gun will malfunction during the inevitable shoot-out with the hero.

Let's look at what happens, mechanically, when a cylinder is swung sharply into the frame in this manner: In most revolvers, cylinder latching is effected by a central pin of relatively small diameter which is powered by a spring. When it's aligned with its mating aperture in the breech face, it snaps in, securing the cylinder in firing position. The heavy cylinder, with the added weight of five or six cartridges, has considerable mass and inertia. When it reaches the alignment point, it's still in motion. The locking pin snaps into its hole, and at the same time impacts against the side of the hole. The pin is normally harder than the frame, so it begins to peen the side of the locking hole. In time, the hole will not be round, but oval. If the cylinder hand slot is on the right side of the gun, the slot may eventually be constricted and bind the cylinder hand. If the ratchet is recessed into the breech face, its edges can be deformed. The delicate timing of the rotation can be affected.

Closing the cylinder of a revolver should be done in the same manner as inserting a pistol magazine—a gentle and firm push, until the latch clicks into place. The really careful shooter who wants to avoid drag marks will even orient the cylinder so the stop is aligned with a locking recess. In certain law enforcement situations, of course, the last point mentioned would be ridiculous. But, if there's no hurry, it will keep your revolver looking new.

Loose Screws

Those who shoot the heavy stuff long ago discovered that the substantial recoil would eventually loosen some or all of the screws. Some manufacturers noted the problem, and I think Ruger was the first to use screws with a transverse nylon pad in the threaded portion of the screw. This added friction and slight springiness which effectively reduced the incidence of loosening, but did not entirely prevent it. Even with nylon-plug screws, an occasional check for tightness is advisable.

To prevent the loosening of ordinary screws, many shooters treat all of them with Loctite, and this will nearly always keep them in place. There are times, though, that total disassembly will be necessary, if only for a yearly major cleaning. When the screws have been treated with a sealant, it makes disassembly an interesting job. I prefer a routine tightening of all screws after each shooting session.

There is another instance of screw loosening that isn't the result of heavy recoil, and any handgun having grip panels of wood is susceptible. As any rifleman knows, stock wood expands and contracts slightly according to atmospheric conditions. The same effect is present in wooden handgun grips. When shrinkage occurs, a screw that was snug will no longer be so. If the grip is loose enough to have perceptible

movement and the gun is fired in this condition, the grip panels may break. So, keep all grip screws snug, but don't over-tighten them.

On most adjustable sights the screws are under spring tension, and this tends to guard against loosening. Click-adjustable types are particularly immune, as they have spring-and-ball detents which bear on the adjustment screws. Some sights, though, have a simple opposed-screw arrangement, and these should be checked every now and then. One revolver screw that is notorious for loosening is the one that retains the ejector housing on guns patterned after the Colt Single Action.

When tightening the screws on any gun, be sure they are snug, but don't overdo it. Firearms screws usually have finer threads than ordinary machine screws, and if too much torque is applied, the screw or its mating threads in the gun may be stripped. On grips, the over-tightening danger is that too much pressure can cause breakage of the grip panels. This is especially true of revolvers that have separate opposed grips, as the center of the grip is often unsupported.

Another grip screw problem can occur in automatics, especially those with grip panels of wood. Over a long period of time, with repeated tightening, the wood beneath the screw heads

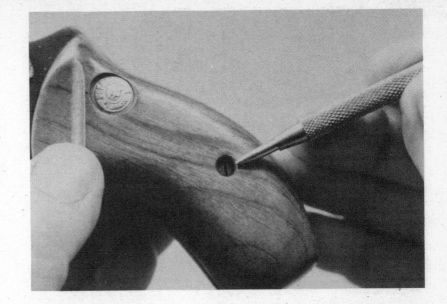

Revolver grip screws are usually centrally-located and the grips are internally unsupported. Over-tightening can crack the grip panels.

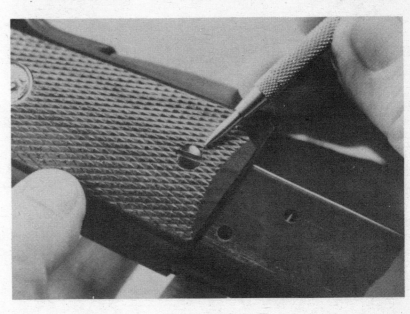

When tightening the grip screws of automatic pistols, keep in mind that altered, replaced, or over-tightened screws can protrude inside the grip frame, damaging the magazine.

can become compressed. This can allow the inside tip of the screw to protrude into the magazine well, or, in some cases, into the operating mechanism. I have seen magazines marked and even dented by protruding grip screws. When tightening the grip screws of automatic pistols, always remove the magazine. Then, if there's a protrusion after tightening, it will be apparent when the magazine is re-inserted.

When this situation is found, it's a simple matter to take out the screws and use a file or a grindstone to remove a little from the screw tips. Some pistols, such as the U.S. Government Model, have separate bushings at each grip screw. As long as the screws and bushings are original and unaltered, no inside protrusion can occur. Sometimes though, shrinkage of the grip panels can cause looseness. An amateur gunsmith will often file the tops of the bushings to correct this, and the result will be protrusion of

Some revolvers and automatics have rear sights that are horizontally adjustable by twin opposed screws, as on this Rossi Model 88. These should be checked often for tightness.

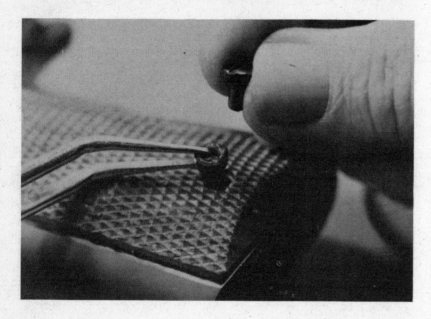

Pistols of Government Model pattern have bushings at each grip screw. When the grips become loose from compression of the grip material, the best way to tighten them is with a small washer of soft plastic or rubber, large enough to encircle the bushing and bear on the grip material.

the screw tips into the magazine well. The right way is to add a thin shim or washer to each screw, encircling the bushing.

The protruding screw tip problem is not limited to grip panel screws. In some cases, other screws can affect mechanical operation in the same way. An example would be the old-style single action revolver. The tip of the screw that retains the combination spring for the trigger and cylinder stop spring can protrude into the cylinder space, and can retard or prevent cylinder rotation. So, when tightening any screw on a handgun, think about where its tip is going. If necessary, shorten the screw.

Revolver Ailments

The revolver is, in general, a delicate beast. An automatic pistol can be so loose that it audibly rattles, and it may still function. A revolver in this condition just stops. The timing of the cylinder rotation is the critical point. The cylinder hand, ratchet, and cylinder stop must all operate in perfect sequence to align the chambers with the firing pin and the barrel. If long use has worn or damaged any of these parts, it's time for a trip to the gunsmith. Revolver timing is not

use of any revolver: To avoid damage, it's best when cocking the hammer for single action firing to draw the hammer back with moderate force.

In most revolvers, as manufactured, the alignment of each cylinder chamber with the bore is almost perfect. The tiny differences covered by that "almost" are normally corrected by the forcing cone, the slightly funneled area at the rear entrance of the barrel. The degree of coning

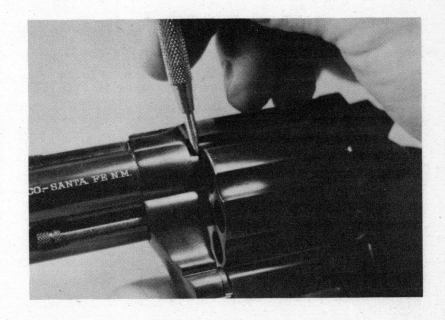

The tool is pointing to the barrel/cylinder gap. If the clearance is very small, and the forcing cone is steeply beveled, there may be a problem when using cast bullets.

tolerant of amateur tinkering.

During the quick-draw craze a few years ago, I saw many single action revolvers that were suffering from chipped and broken cylinder stops, and deformation of the stop slots on the cylinders. The game required that the hammer be racked back sharply as the gun was brought into firing position, and this resulted in rather violent engagement between the stop and its slots. Transferring this information to ordinary

varies widely, and some revolvers benefit from having the forcing cone minimally increased and polished. This requires special tools, and the services of a gunsmith.

Some revolvers have a very close fit between the front of the cylinder and the rear face of the barrel. When this is combined with a minimal cone, and when lead or alloy cast bullets are used, the shaving that occurs can stop the cylinder rotation. The remedy is to slightly enlarge

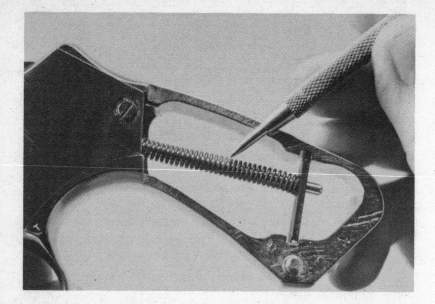

When custom-tuning a handgun, it's not a good idea to alter the original springs by reshaping or removing a few coils. On the Colt Mark V shown, a factory-length hammer spring already provides a superb trigger pull.

Gas cutting in revolvers is not unusual, nor is it a cause for concern. On the 32-20 Smith & Wesson Model 1905 shown, many years of shooting produced a tiny groove above the barrel.

both the cone and the barrel/cylinder gap. The flash may be a little more pronounced, but the gas loss has been proved by testing to be so small that it is not of any real significance.

In tuning revolvers for competition or personal defense use, there is one alteration often done that is not a good idea: lightening of the hammer and trigger springs to give an easier double action trigger pull. Sometimes this is done by altering the original springs, and some-

times by installing one of the available spring kits. The kits may work well on one particular gun, and may cause misfires on another gun of the same type. If you use one of these, it's best to try it out extensively—before relying on it in competition or defense.

Altering the original springs is nearly always a bad move. In time, misfires are almost sure to develop, and in some situations this could have serious consequences. If you want a silky-

A typical top-break revolver. This one, a very late-production Iver Johnson, is chambered for the 32 S&W Long cartridge.

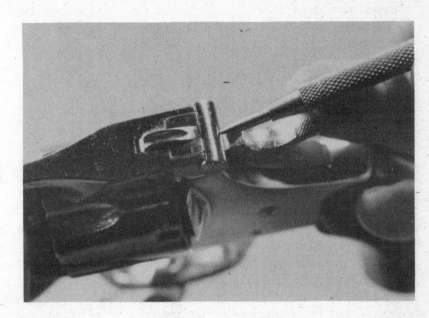

The tool indicates the "T-latch" of a typical top-break revolver. This type of latching system is suitable only for low-pressure cartridges.

smooth double action trigger pull, have a good pistolsmith polish all of the mating surfaces in the action, and leave the springs alone. Or, you could just buy a Colt Python. Its legendary smoothness is due to a lot of hand-fitting and polishing, and this is one of the reasons for its substantial cost.

With the introduction of the 357 Maximum cartridge, and its subsequent revolver problems, a lot of shooters learned a new term: "gas-cut-ting." It's an effect that has always been present in most revolvers, and the Maximum round just made it more noticeable: Escaping gas will eventually cut a shallow groove on the underside of the frame topstrap, just above the barrel/cylinder gap. In some revolvers, a groove is machined at that point during manufacturing. Alloy-frame guns often have a steel insert in that location. The obvious concern has been that the cutting would weaken the topstrap. It's been found, though, that for some unknown reason the gas cutting will go only so far, and then will stop; continued firing will not deepen the groove. With the Maximum round, there was also another problem—erosion of the barrel cone. In most revolvers, though, some minor gas cutting is normal, and it's nothing to worry about.

There are large numbers of old top-break revolvers that are still in use as personal protection pieces in homes and businesses, so I'm adding a few words on them here. There is nothing basically wrong with the top-break design—Webley of England made revolvers of this type that were virtually indestructible, and several of them were used for many years as standard British military sidearms. The Webley difference was in its superior barrel latch.

The older U.S. top-breaks, by Smith & Wesson, Iver Johnson, and others, all had the same weakness: a relatively small T-shaped latch that engaged vertical posts on the frame. Even with the mild loads that these guns chambered, such as the 32 and 38 S&W rounds, this latching arrangement would eventually loosen, and sometimes break. Besides being of inadequate proportions, the T-latch also had poor mechanical advantage in relation to the direction of the applied forces.

Modern high-pressure loads spelled the end of the T-latch top-break. If you have one of these guns, check the barrel latch for tightness. If it's loose, there are ways it can be tightened—see your gunsmith. With the use of mild factory loads, and proper maintenance, there's no reason these guns can't continue to be used for protection. Their cartridges are weak by today's standards, but in most situations they will probably be adequate.

Auto Pistols—a Final Mechanical Note

A colleague whose opinions I respect recently told me that the slide of an empty automatic shouldn't be allowed to slam closed, as this could cause possible damage. His reasoning was the same as that applied to dry-firing. According to his idea, the stripping of a cartridge from the magazine and its chambering would have the same cushioning effect on the slide, barrel, and other parts as the primer or snap-cap has on the firing pin. So, he said, the slide of an empty auto should be eased forward, not just dropped by tripping the slide latch. To be honest, I'm not sure about this one. The principal impact strain of slide return is on whatever retains the barrel in the frame. In most Browning-pattern pistols, this would be the cross-shaft of the slide latch. In this instance, there's no question of crystallization or peening, just strength.

In guns of the type mentioned, this cross-shaft has an important role in the locking system, and in this it is subjected to far more stress than it receives by the impact of slide return. Is the slide actually slowed enough by the action of cartridge pick-up and chambering to make a measurable difference in its closing impact? I think I'll leave this one up to the feelings of the individual shooter. Speaking for myself, I still trip the latch and drop the slide.

Carrying

For those who frequently carry a handgun, in law enforcement, security work, or as a licensed private citizen, there should be two main considerations: *Accessability,* and *Safety.* Some of the very small guns have long been known as "pocket pistols," but even with the tiny 22 and 25 caliber handguns, a holster is best. I have been involved as a technical witness in several cases in which a gun fell from a pocket and caused injury. There is a wide choice of holsters

For really safe carrying, all handguns should be in holsters. This applies even to those considered to be pocket pistols. The excellent 25 Seecamp double action is shown with three fine holsters made by Strong: A "billfold" type, an inside-the-belt (or trousers) model, and a snap-on belt-slide.

dental firing is unlikely. I don't say "impossible," because even the best safety system can fail or malfunction.

Single action revolvers are still much-used for sporting purposes, and in recent years a number of them have been re-designed to incorporate hammer block and transfer bar systems. For those, the remarks above apply. There are, though, large numbers of old style single action guns that are still in use. One friend of mine,

for every handgun, and it's not difficult to choose the best type for a particular application.

When the gun carried is a modern double action revolver, there is no question about a safe carrying mode. All currently-made DA revolvers have some form of automatic internal safety, utilizing either a hammer block or a transfer bar, and these can be safely carried with all chambers loaded. Even if the gun is dropped, or the hammer is struck by some external object, acci-

who uses an old style Super Blackhawk frequently, insists that the action is superior to the New Model gun. He, of course, carries his 44 Magnum with only five chambers loaded, and the hammer fully down on an empty chamber.

Even an illiterate cowboy of the last century knew that this is the *only* way to safely carry an old-style single action, but in today's product liability jungle, revolvers of this type have been the subject of many lawsuits. In all of the acci-

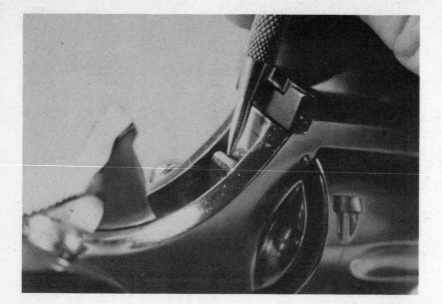

In the Colt Mark V revolver, the tool is pointing to the transfer bar, which is elevated to this point only when the trigger is at the rear. Several modern revolvers use this system.

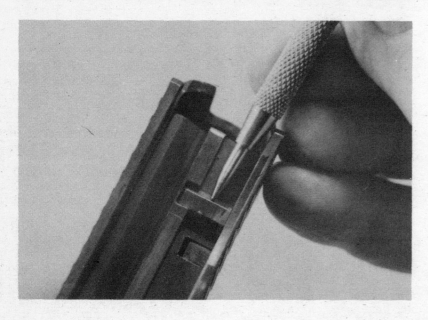

Looking at the underside of the slide of a SIG/Sauer P220, the tool indicates the automatic firing pin block.

dent cases I have examined, the owner of the gun did something unwise, such as carrying it with the hammer fully down on a loaded chamber. A firearm is a potentially dangerous tool or item of sporting equipment, in the same category as a power saw or a baseball bat. If you do something foolish with it, someone can get hurt.

Modern automatic pistols, especially double action guns in the more expensive group, often have firing pin block safety systems, and some

of these are entirely automatic in their operation. The usual form has the block cleared by the last fraction of rearward trigger movement. This is a good system, and if it's in proper working order, no manual safety is necessary if the gun has an external hammer. In these guns, the carrying mode should be with the chamber loaded and the hammer fully down.

Because of its long use as the U.S. military pistol and its reputation for dependability, the

The hammer of this Colt Mark IV Series 70 pistol is shown in the so-called "half-cock" position. This step on the hammer is designed to catch it if the thumb slips during cocking. It is *not* a safety position.

Government Model is one of the most popular automatics for competitive sport shooting and personal defense. Recently, in their Series 80 version, Colt added an automatic firing pin block safety to the design. The Arminex Trifire has a manual firing pin block safety. Except for these two, all true GM-pattern pistols have a manual sear-block safety. For many years (perhaps still?) the prescribed military carrying mode has been with the magazine fully loaded and the chamber empty. Presumably, in battle situations, this rule was not strongly enforced.

Among today's serious competitive shooters, the chosen mode is usually "cocked-and-locked"—that is, with the chamber loaded, the hammer cocked, and the manual safety engaged. My friend Jeff Cooper named this "Condition One," and its safety factor is often reinforced by the use of a holster having a strap that crosses between the cocked hammer and the firing pin. The safety record of those using this mode of carry is impressive, but it still makes me uneasy.

For this type of gun, I would choose what Jeff calls "Condition Two"—with the chamber loaded and the hammer fully down. True, this mode may be just a little slower to get into operation, but I feel better when I have more control

of putting the gun into a fire-capable status. With the hammer down and the firing pin an inertia-type, even an external impact on the hammer is unlikely to cause accidental firing. By the way, this might be a good place to point out that the so-called "half-cock" on the GM-pattern pistol is *not* a carrying safety, and it was never intended to be. It's there to catch the hammer if the thumb slips during cocking.

It just occurred to me that sometimes those of us who write about firearms may use terms that may puzzle readers who are not experienced gun people. A term like "firing pin block" is fairly self-explanatory, but what about an "inertia firing pin?" Since I used the term in the paragraph above, perhaps a quick definition is in order: An inertia-type firing pin is one that is not long enough to reach the primer of a chambered cartridge when the hammer is fully down. When struck by the hammer, its inertia carries it forward, against light spring tension, to reach the primer. By comparison, a non-inertia or full-reach firing pin protrudes from the breech face when the hammer is down.

Many of the older external-hammer single action automatics, and a few of the double actions, have full-reach firing pins. To check for this, with the slide locked open or taken off the gun,

To check for a full-reach or inertia firing pin, open the slide and hold a straight-edged object to depress the head of the pin even with the rear edge of its tunnel. If the firing pin point protrudes from the breech face, then it's a full-reach firing pin. If it stays within its aperture, it's an inertia type.

hold a straight-edged object such as a steel ruler against the firing pin head, depressing it even with the rear edge of its slide tunnel. Holding it there, check for protrusion of its tip at the breech face. If the tip is not entirely within its aperture in the breech face, then it's a full-reach pin. Guns of this type will usually have a "safety step" position on the hammer, keeping it away from the firing pin head. If so, this should be used for carrying. If not, it's sometimes possible to convert the firing pin to an inertia type. Ask your gunsmith.

Cases

I am intentionally avoiding getting into the specific types of holsters, because the great variety of styles would fill a book in itself. I will comment, though, on the different carrying cases that are available, because the number of basic types is not as large, and not much has been written about them. They range from the simple gun sock to the fine hard cases in heavy plastic and aluminum.

Some years ago at a gun show, I bought a half-dozen gun socks that were made by some enterprising dealer (or his wife) from blanket material. They are simply two triangular pieces of heavy fabric, stitched together on their long sides, with the large end left open. I still use them occasionally, to keep several handguns from knocking together in the range box. By themselves they're not suitable for carrying—there's no way to close the open end, other than folding it over.

Next up the scale from these are the commercially-made sheaths that have an integral set of tie-thongs at the end. These are usually made of either a suede-like fabric or a soft plastic material, and a few have now begun to appear in nylon. They offer somewhat more carrying security than the simple "sock," but their main utility is still as separators within a range box or other larger case.

The familiar half-oval zipper case is perhaps the minimum type for separate carrying. These are made of soft plastic, canvas, or leather, and

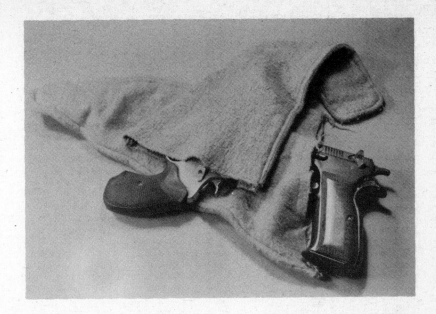

These gun socks, home-made of blanket material, were purchased at a gun show. For separating handguns within a larger case, they serve their purpose.

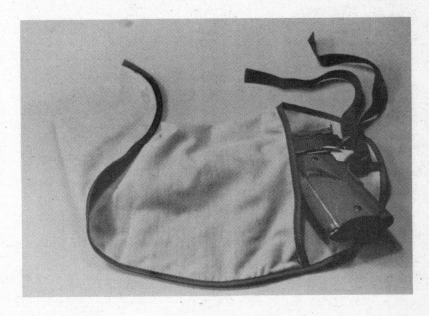

A similar idea to the gun sock is this Outers Gun Sheath, a much more professional rendition. It has a closing flap with ties, and is made of soft flannel fabric that is treated with silicone.

are usually lined with either flannel or a fur-like material. An improvement on the basic zipper case is a rectangular version with carrying handles. A further improvement, recently introduced by Bob Allen, is a case of this type with an internal pocket that contains a packet of absorbent silica gel. Any moisture that enters is taken up by the packet, and kept off the surfaces of the gun. This is a welcome innovation, because humidity can be a problem in any closed case, especially in those with a solid plastic exterior. With the exception of the Bob Allen case mentioned above, these cases should not be used for handgun storage over long periods of time. They're fine, though, for transporting handguns to the range. Their only disadvantage is that they are one-gun cases.

When more than one gun is involved, it's best to step up to the top level, the hard cases. These are usually fully lined with foam rubber in an

The familiar oval zipper cases are usually lined with sheepskin or flannel, and have exteriors of vinyl, canvas, or leather.

A step upward in the single-gun case is this Gun Shield by Bob Allen. It has a double zipper and carrying handles. The material is a tough nylon.

egg-carton or waffle pattern, to gently but firmly grip the guns and keep them from touching. In the hard plastic type, I often use a Gun Guard case by Doskocil. It has a full piano-type hinge and double latches that lock with a key. The plastic outer shell is thick, and these cases are virtually indestructible.

The Outers division of Omark Industries recently began production of what may be the ultimate hard case. They call it the Silverline, an obvious reference to the color of its satin-finish aluminum exterior. The aluminum used is not thin, and its seamless, rounded contours give ample strength without a lot of weight. The interior is the usual interlocking-pattern foam rubber, and there are several nice design touches. The Silverline case has a full-length piano-type hinge, and the hinge is internally shielded with foam rubber. The meeting edges are covered by a welt of soft rubber, to seal the case against

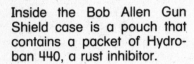
Inside the Bob Allen Gun Shield case is a pouch that contains a packet of Hydroban 440, a rust inhibitor.

The well-made hard plastic Gun Guard case by Doskocil is made in several sizes. It has twin lockable latches and a piano-type hinge, and is lined in waffle foam rubber.

dust or wet weather. There's a strong and fully-recessed lock with a machine-cut key.

These Outers cases have an airline-approved luggage rating, and look as if they'd survive the gorilla-treatment of that famous TV commercial. One of the outstanding points that I particularly noticed are the four little feet that the case rests on when standing. They're not plastic or rubber, but solid, turned aluminum. The case is listed by Outers as having a two-gun capacity,

but I've found that its 13 by 18-inch dimensions will easily contain four large-frame automatics. A free silicon-treated sheath comes with each case, and the price is very reasonable.

From this briefcase-style carrier, the next logical item is a case that shooters usually refer to as a "range box," a case that will not only transport handguns, but also ammunition and other accessories. In this category, there are some very elaborate (and expensive) cases avail-

The handsome Silverline case by Outers has an exterior of seamless aluminum, and a rubber sealed edge that protects against the weather. It has twin latches, and a single machined-key lock.

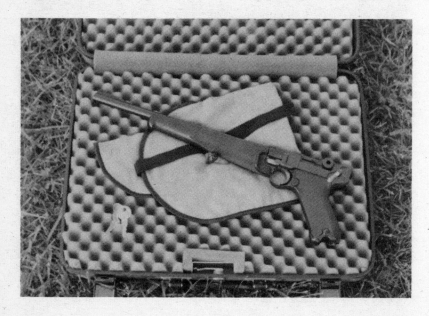

The foam rubber interior of the Silverline case has deep waffles, and the piano-type hinge is covered by a foam rubber shield. An Outers Gun Sheath comes with each case.

able. Some of these are beautifully made, and have such nice features as padded racks that hold guns vertically, in a row. Unfortunately, cases of this type are usually priced beyond the financial reach of the average shooter.

For the people who drive pickup trucks rather than Porsches (and I include myself in this group) it's good news that there are now range boxes made of tough, space-age plastics. They're almost indestructible, and in comparison with the old-style boxes, their cost is very reasonable. They also have other advantages: The plastic is naturally rain-proof, and there are no exposed metal parts that might mar the finish of a prized handgun. Both of the cases that I use most often are this type.

One is designed particularly for the Thompson/Center Contender, and its lift-out tray is recessed to hold a Contender pistol with a barrel length of up to 14 inches, with a scope attached.

This is The Container, made of blow-moulded polyethylene by the Airmold Division of W. R. Grace & Co.

The Container is designed specifically for the Thompson/ Center Contender, but it will also accommodate other handguns. The lid is lined with foam rubber, and there is a large compartment under the tray.

There is also a separate recess in the tray for an extra barrel. Below the tray, the bottom of the case has ample room for ammunition, accessories, or other guns. While the case is made for the Contender, it could be used for any handgun. This case is made of high-density blow-molded polyethylene, with double-wall construction. It's called The Container, from the Airmold Division, W. R. Grace & Company, Box 610, Roanoke Rapids, NC 27870.

The other "box" is one that goes to the range with me every time. It's the Paac Case by West Ohio Gun Company, Incorporated, P-685 Rd. 16, Route Two, Napoleon, Ohio 43545. This case is made of an extremely tough ABS plastic, and it has so many good features that it's difficult to put them in any sort of order. There's a full-length piano-type hinge with a completely-enclosed steel rod insert, and the lid has the same dimensions as the bottom, so the case

The Paac Case, by West Ohio Gun Company, is a fine range box made of tough ABS plastic. Its carrying handle folds into a recess, and it has twin sliding latches that will take small padlocks.

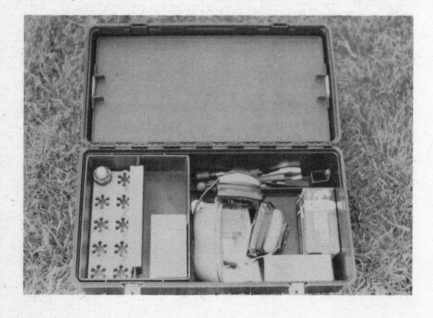

The Paac Case opens out flat, and its full-length hinge has a steel-rod insert. The lower portion is compartmented for tools and accessories.

opens flat. Inside the lid, there's a lock-in removable tray. The inside of the lid and the underside of the tray are covered in interlocking foam rubber, and this is where the guns are carried. The bottom has three divided compartments. On the right side, a large compartment will hold earmuffs, shooting glasses, and so on. To the rear of this, a narrow compartment is perfect for tools. On the left, there's a large ammunition storage compartment, and a fitted lift-out tray with a retractable handle. The tray is divided into two long compartments, for live ammo and fired cases. Fitted into the "live" side is a speedloader filler block with a capacity of 60 rounds (ten loaders). The gun compartment will hold four handguns with 6-inch barrels, and one or two more if they're shorter. This is absolutely the finest case of its type I have seen, and it must have been designed by a shooter. There are other nice little features: The

Removing the tray in the lid of the Paac Case reveals a handgun-storage compartment lined in waffle foam. The tray locks in place, holding the guns firmly. The removable compartment on the left has two sections and a pull-up handle. Note the insert that will hold ten speedloaders.

This is the large #1175 Duffle Bag by Special Weapons Products. Made of heavy Cordura nylon, it has a large main compartment and three external zipper-closed pouches.

carrying handle folds into a recess when not in use, and the twin lid latches have holed flanges for two padlocks, if you should want to add them. Finally, the case is guaranteed against defects in material and workmanship for one year. I've used mine for longer than that, and it still looks like new.

In recent times, there has been a trend in holsters and cases toward the use of Cordura nylon, a Du Pont product. The stuff is extremely resis-tant to wear and tearing, and for those who prefer a soft range case, there are several makers offering them. One that I often use is the large Duffle Bag (#1175) by Special Weapons Products, Building 601, Space Center, Mira Loma, California 91752. Its exterior is made of waterproof 11-ounce Cordura nylon. It measures 11 by 12 by 22 inches, and will contain an amazing amount of equipment. I've carried a Bushmaster pistol, a Wilkinson Linda pistol, several large

All of the large handguns and other items shown fit easily into the Special Weapons Bag, with room to spare. For shooters who prefer a soft range bag, this one is perfect.

Inexpensive but extremely tough, these shooting glasses by Hoppe's are made of high-impact polycarbonate and have integral side-shields.

conventional handguns, a considerable amount of ammunition, earmuffs, shooting glasses, tools, and other items, and still had space to spare.

This bag has a large main compartment and three separate external pouches, all closed by high-quality YKK zippers with rain flaps. The zippers on the main compartment and the long side pouch have double tabs, and can be opened in either direction. At one end, there is an extra zippered compartment with a waterproof nylon bag that extends into the main compartment, useful for items that you want to keep separated. In the event that this bag is used for travel, rather than as a range case, this compartment would also be useful for soiled clothing. The comfortable carrying handle has a rolled center piece with a Velcro seal that joins the two loops, and this is unfastened for complete access to the main compartment. The nylon straps of the car-

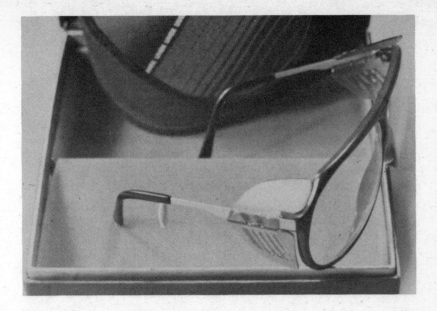

The Bilsom shooting glasses by Uvex are of high quality, and are available with lenses of clear, grey, or yellow polycarbonate. The temple pieces are steel, and they are equipped with side-shields.

One of the best hearing protectors on the market is the Bilsom Viking. It has a foam-padded back-frame and a soft plastic strap that goes over the head.

rying loops also extend entirely around the bottom of the bag, an important strength factor. The bag comes in brown, black, and camouflage-pattern, and the price at the time this is written is around $45. There are other bags that may equal its features, but none will surpass it.

Two of the items that go into these equipment cases should be mentioned in more detail. Among all the items for handgun care, we shouldn't forget two care accessories that apply to the shooter himself: Protection for the eyes and ears. As most shooters have come to realize, those who don't ordinarily wear eyeglasses should always wear some type of shooting glasses.

Sometimes, even those who *do* wear prescription glasses will need shooting glasses. My own case is an example. I use two different sets of glasses, one for very close shop work, the other for distance viewing. Neither is right for a clear

A very good moderately-priced earmuff is this one by Silencio, the pair shown marked with the name of my friendly local gun shop.

view of the sights on a handgun. So, in my range box, I have two pairs of plain, non-corrective shooting glasses. Both are in the yellow tint that I prefer, but it should be noted that most shooting glasses are also available with grey or clear lenses.

My shooting glasses are examples of a price range from very inexpensive to medium-expensive. In the former category, they are Hoppe's (#3070), made entirely of a tough, high-impact polycarbonate that gives a distortion-free view. The temple hinges are of steel and there are integral side-shields, for complete protection from powder gases or any other hazards. Even though they are inexpensive, they comply with the optical and safety requirements of the American Standard Association Safety Code. You can find these glasses at any gun shop that carries Hoppe's products. Or, you can write to Hoppe's Division, Penguin Industries, Airport Industrial Mall, Coatesville, Pennsylvania 19320.

My other glasses are the superb Uvex, marketed by Bilsom International, 11800 Sunrise Valley Drive, Reston, Virginia 22091. The Bilsom name for these glasses is Rangemaster, and in yellow they're Model #1161. The lenses, also offered in grey, are heavy polycarbonate, and easily pass the A. N. S. I. standard. The

temple pieces are steel, with comfortable plastic ear hooks, and there are plastic side-shields. The temple hinges are of steel, screw-mounted on the frame. The glasses come with a nylon case that has a belt snap-loop and a Velcro closure. When you examine these glasses, the quality is obvious.

For the first 20 years of my association with firearms, I didn't even think of the effect of all those explosions on my ears. Now, I find that I can't hear some things, such as the weird chirping ring of some modern telepones. To save the hearing I have left, I always use some type of hearing protector. One set, by Silencio, was given to me by Lock & Load Gun Shop of Evansville, Indiana, and it hangs on the rifle rack in my truck—for times when I don't have my range box.

In the box, my main set of earmuffs is the Viking #2318 by Bilsom AB of Billesholm, Sweden, marketers of the Uvex glasses described earlier. These are the most comfortable and effective muffs I've ever used. The official EPA noise reduction rating is figured from 0 to 30, and the Viking is rated at 28. I prefer the behind-the-head position, and these muffs have an extra feature for this: It's an adjustable strap of soft plastic that goes over the top of the head, and is thin enough that it doesn't interfere with a hat. This high-quality hearing protector is priced only a little higher than most other well-known brands.

The glasses and hearing protectors mentioned above happen to be the ones that I use, but there are several other excellent brands available. In hearing protectors, for example, I've tried in-the-ear devices by Lee Engineering, and my extra set of muffs for friends who forget to bring theirs along are by David Clark. When you select a set of hearing protectors, keep in mind the EPA numbers mentioned earlier, and arrive at a compromise between the most effective sound reduction and wearing comfort.

Safety

By now, most shooters are familiar with the "Ten Commandments of Safety" that were first proposed, I think, by someone at SAAMI—the Sporting Arms and Ammunition Manufacturers Institute. Variations of this list of safety rules have been repeated by the National Rifle Association, the National Shooting Sports Foundation, and others. For those who may have joined us late, I'll list them again here:

1. Treat every gun with the respect due a loaded gun.

2. Carry only empty guns, taken down or with the action open, into your automobile, camp, or home.

3. Always be sure that the barrel and action are clear of obstructions.

4. Always carry your gun so that you can control the direction of the muzzle even if you stumble.

5. Be sure of your target before you pull the trigger.

6. Never point a gun at anything you do not want to shoot.

7. Never leave your gun unattended unless you unload it first.

8. Never climb a tree or a fence with a loaded gun.

9. Never shoot at a flat hard surface or the surface of water.

10. Do not mix gunpowder and alcohol.

Well, when applied strictly to hunting or target shooting, these are pretty good rules. Number eight has always amused me—I can imagine a hunter, pursued by a farmer's mean bull, stopping to unload his gun before climbing over the fence. . . . In the area of personal protection, though, a couple of these rules make no sense at all. When you are awakened by strange noises in your home at night, it's no time to be fumbling with ammunition. On the other hand, loaded handguns can't be left lying around the house, especially in homes where there are children. At first glance, this would seem to be a problem without a solution, but actually, it's not that difficult. It can be solved in two ways: By instruction, and by your choice of home-defense handguns.

Also, there are some safety devices that are helpful. The first of these noted here is useful only if those handling the firearms have had some instruction, or at least are capable of reading a warning. For pre-school children, it would be less effective. It's called the "Tattle-Tale," and it's made by the J. R. Stupero Company,

The Tattle-Tale is a little red plastic tag that will snap onto the trigger guard of any handgun. It won't prevent firing, but it will warn the forgetful.

The Gun Lock by Master Lock Company has been around for quite a while, and it's very effective. When installed as shown, the handgun can't be fired until a machine-cut key is used to remove the lock.

Box 155, Lakeville, Minnesota 55044. This is an inexpensive little clip of red plastic that easily snaps on the trigger guard of any pistol or revolver, and its two rectangular sides are plainly marked in white: "CAUTION: LOADED FIREARM." While it does not prevent the gun from being fired, it does offer a reminder for those who might forget.

The Master Lock Company of Milwaukee, Wisconsin offers the Model 90 Gun Lock, and it *will* prevent unauthorized operation. This device fits over the entire trigger guard of most handguns, and locks with a removable key. Padded inside with soft rubber, it will not mar the finest gun. When it's installed on a double action handgun, with its locking crossbolt behind the trigger, the gun can't even be cocked. Master locks have an excellent reputation, and this unit is well-made. If you plan to apply them to more than one gun, you can arrange to have all the

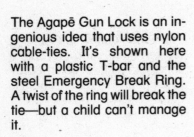
The Agapē Gun Lock is an ingenious idea that uses nylon cable-ties. It's shown here with a plastic T-bar and the steel Emergency Break Ring. A twist of the ring will break the tie—but a child can't manage it.

locks operate with the same key.

The company recommends, of course, that the lock not be used on loaded guns. Even so, this would be one way to cancel the ammo-fumbling in the night syndrome. You'd still have to find and insert the key, but this would be quicker and less complicated than loading in the dark. The Master Gun Lock is a very effective safety device. When it's properly in place, the gun cannot be fired. It costs less than $10.

Another device, recently introduced, is the Agapē Gun Lock. It utilizes nylon cable ties, and, in some applications, plastic T-blocks. It's not for use on loaded guns, as it requires that the slide be opened on autos, and the cylinder swung out on revolvers. An "emergency break ring" is provided, and it can be twisted to break the nylon tie—but not by a child. Sixty pounds of force will break the tie, and it's easy for most adults, but small children can't manage it. There are two Agapē kits available. One has ten ties and a break ring, and the other has the same items plus three of the T-blocks. Both kits are extremely inexpensive, and they're obtainable from Agapē Gun Lock, Incorporated, Box 11, Belmont, Michigan 49306. Bill Bayn, the man who came up with this ingenious idea, is a 25-year veteran of the Michigan State Police.

Finally, there's the best of the home-safety handgun devices, the Gunsafe, made by Lasco, Incorporated, West 35 Main Avenue, Spokane, Washington 99201. The gun can be kept fully loaded, nestled securely in foam rubber, and secured inside a locked box of heavy-gauge steel. The lid overlaps the bottom part, making the box nearly impossible to pry open. Best of all, there's no key. The lock is a push-button combination type that comes preset to three digits. There are five buttons, and the owner can reset the lock at any time to a new combination of up to five digits. The box measures 8 by 12 by 4 inches, and it will fit into the drawer of most bedside tables. Or, it can be left in plain view, because it doesn't *look* like a gun case. It's also small enough that it can easily be carried in a car, camper, or boat. Once the combination is learned, it can be opened in less than 5 seconds, even in the dark. The quality of this little "safe" is high, and it's medium-expensive, selling for around $70 at the time this is written. It's definitely worth the price. My downstairs gun, a 45 caliber Heckler & Koch P9S, is resting in one right now.

All four of the devices mentioned have value, but let's get back to the original problem. In homes where there are children, and where a

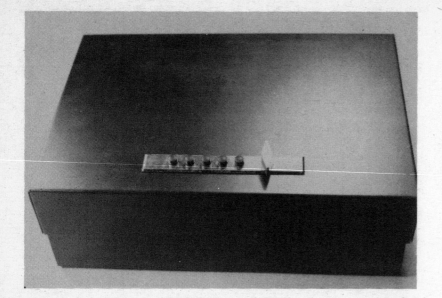

The steel Lasco Gunsafe is an excellent idea. It has a combination lock actuated by five push-buttons, and is easily opened in the dark if you know the sequence.

Inside, the Lasco Gunsafe is lined in foam rubber, and holds the handgun securely. Its overlapping edges make unauthorized access virtually impossible.

handgun is kept for protection, the child or children must be taught from an early age the rules of proper handling. When this is done in the right way, it accomplishes three things. It satisfies the child's natural inquisitiveness about firearms, removing the element of mystery. It imparts the skill of safe firearms operation. And, it introduces the child to a fine sport. With proper instruction, it's possible to have children and loaded guns in a home, with no accidents.

For those who may be upset by that last remark, I will note that I have five children, four of whom are still at home. Their ages range from 11 to 24. There has never been even a *near* accident. Perhaps those three words in the paragraph above should have been emphasized: *With proper instruction*—it works. Now, this is fine for your own children, but what about their friends, who have not had safe-handling instruction? Well, this brings us to the second part of

The author's bedside gun is this Ruger Speed Six, equipped with a factory spurless hammer and Sile walnut grips. With the absence of a hammer spur, small children could not operate it.

In the automatics, one relatively child-safe pistol is the excellent 9mm Heckler & Koch P7. Small hands would lack the span and strength to depress its cocking lever.

the answer: Your choice of guns.

Some modern handguns, such as the beautiful Colt Python, have superbly smooth actions. Even if a youngster lacked the hand-span to operate a handgun of this type in double action mode, it would be easy to cock the external hammer for single action firing. So, the choice here is obvious: Select a home-defense handgun that would be difficult or impossible for children to operate, but one that could be easily used by

an adult. Here's an example: In the bookcase-headboard of my bed is a Ruger Speed-Six revolver with the optional spurless hammer. The small hands of my daughter's children simply cannot make it function, and my own children would never touch it. Needless to say, their friends are not allowed in the master bedroom, and it's locked when we're not there.

An even more effective alternative choice might be to choose an automatic pistol having a fairly strong recoil spring, load the magazine, and leave the chamber empty. Small hands couldn't manipulate the slide, but an adult could easily cycle it when an emergency occurred. Another alternate plan would be to keep the loaded magazine and the pistol in separate but easily accessible locations.

It occurs to me that there is one modern automatic that could even be safe around small children with the chamber loaded: The Heckler & Koch P7. It is uncocked at all times, with the firing pin locked, except when its squeeze-cocking lever that forms the frontstrap of the grip frame is fully depressed. This requires a positive grip by an adult-sized hand. I doubt that any

small child could manage it, even if both hands were used. I hasten to add that this is my opinion, not Heckler & Koch's!

In all of the examples and suggestions noted above, though, I recognize that there may be exceptions. Some very young children might be stronger than average for their size and age. So, each gun owner must determine this factor, and plan accordingly. When the guns in question are strictly for target or hunting use, by all means, put them under lock and key. Store the ammunition separately. This will serve a dual purpose: It will keep them out of the hands of inexperienced people, and it will made them less accessible to thieves.

Storage

In regard to the possibility of theft, there are several ways to address this potential problem. I've often heard suggestions that gun owners, especially those who own several guns, should not display them in glass-front cases in the home. In some cities, and in some areas of the country, this is probably good advice. There's no point in inviting thieves by displaying guns where they can be seen through windows, from outside. Some advisers go even further, and say that owners should never show their prized pieces to friends or anyone else, lest it become known that they have valuable guns on the premises.

For the collector, hunter, or target shooter, perhaps both of these suggestions are good ones. I'll admit, though, that I don't subscribe to either of them. Some of my handguns are in a glass case on the wall behind my office desk, and my office is in my home. Also, since I am fairly well-known in my area as a ''gun person,'' it would be ridiculous to pretend that there are no firearms in my house. Yet, in the 30 years I have lived in this vicinity, there has never been even an attempt at theft.

I think this is due to several factors. First of all, I'm not a collector, handgun hunter, or target shooter. My shooting is combat-style, and since I have been a consultant to various law enforcement and security agencies in that capacity, there is public knowledge of this. In my home at night, I'm definitely not paranoid about the possibility of a break-in—I'm just ready. Also, my preferred working hours are a little strange, usually from around 8 or 9 o'clock in the evening to 3 or 4 in the morning. And, I have three good watchdogs outside. In the house, there's a Dachshund who imagines herself a vicious Doberman. If someone does get in, I can deal with him while he's trying to convince Fröliche to remove her teeth from his ankle.

Unfortunately, most of these factors could not be applied to the average gun owner. For many, the ultimate security against theft is a safe, such as those offered by Cannon, Fort Knox, Browning, Outers and others. For those who can afford their substantial cost, these vaults will certainly prevent theft by the ordinary break-in artist. There are some, though, who would be only temporarily deterred by even the most sophisticated safe. Still, in a burglary, any delay is a good thing. It might cause the furtive visitors to give up and leave, or stay long enough to be caught.

For those of us who can't afford the heavy vaults, there's a lighter and far less expensive unit that is lockable and offers good protection as a delaying factor in case of a burglary, as well as keeping guns away from unauthorized persons or children. It's made by Medart, Incorporated, Box 658, Greenwood, Mississippi 38930, a firm that also makes those tough lockers for schools. The Deluxe unit, the one that I have, has space in the lower part for six rifles or shotguns, a shelf at the top, and an inner compartment with a separate door. Both the main door and the compartment door have latches with padlock eyes. The shelf and the compartment are perfect for handguns and ammunition.

While this is no vault, it's certainly not flimsy. The door is of 18-gauge sheet steel, the frame is 16-gauge, and the body parts are 24-gauge. The finish is electrostatic baked-on enamel. The barrel rest for the long guns is plastic-covered, and the floor of the cabinet is covered in a plastic carpet-like material. The unit is 72 inches tall, 18 inches wide, and 12 inches deep. It comes disassembled, and I was surprised to find that all of the parts were there, and all of the fittings and holes aligned perfectly. Best of all, it costs less than $200, including shipping charges. In its price range, there is no better gun locker on the market.

Whether guns are stored in this good locker, a closet, or a heavy safe, moisture can be a problem in some areas of the country. The more airtight the enclosure, the more likely that condensation will occur. There are active dehumidifiers that run on electricity, but most of these are designed for rooms, and will not fit in a gun cabinet. While there is some advantage in lowering the humidity of the room, it's best to have the dehumidifying effect closer to the items stored. For this, the accepted material is silica gel. It works best in tightly enclosed areas, and is the

dessicant used by museums, industry, and the U.S. government.

The usual form is in containers of various sizes, to be used in relation to the size of the area involved. The containers are of ventilated metal, or are cloth bags, sometimes within a vented cardboard box. Most containers feature an indicator that changes color as the silica reaches its saturation point. It can then be removed and dried in an ordinary kitchen oven. If the instructions are exactly followed, the units can be used over and over, indefinitely.

I have tried two units from the Hydrosorbent Company, Box 675, Rye, New York 10580. One is a 40-gram metal-cased type that's suitable for small areas, such as a drawer in a gun cabinet. The other is a 360-gram unit, a cloth bag in a perforated cardboard box, and this one will protect 27 cubic feet of area, comparable to the size of a small gun cabinet or safe. The company also offers units in other sizes, including a monster 2000-gram cylindrical metal type that will protect 144 cubic feet of space.

The other units I have used are by Rust Patrol, 6245 Rosier Road, Canandaigua, New York 14424. They have a small metal-cased unit that is virtually identical to the one described above, and their next larger unit is contained in a cloth drawstring bag, to protect an area of 25 to 30 cubic feet. They also offer a smaller disposable bag, without indicator, that is very low-priced. This one is designed to be used in a drawer for a specified length of time, and then thrown away. It would be possible, though, to open the top of the bag and reactivate the crystals with heat, just as in the larger containers.

It should be pointed out that none of these units can dehumidify the entire outdoor world. The more tightly the enclosure is sealed, the longer they will last. If humidity conditions are high, and the storage space is opened frequently, then reactivation will have to be done more often. Also, when a unit is first used, it may deactivate more quickly than in later use. This is because it will take up any residual moisture in the wood of a cabinet, drawer linings, etc.

Alarm Devices

Returning for a moment to the idea of theft prevention, let's consider the use of electronic detection devices. There are, of course, some very sophisticated alarm systems available, both in-house types and those that are connected to security or law enforcement agencies. These are excellent, but can be *very* expensive. Because of this factor, I had originally intended to omit alarms and similar detection systems from this discussion, as most are priced beyond the means

each unit. In normal use, they will last about a year. The Owl is not a plastic toy, it's a heavy, well-made device of high quality.

There is a siren-type speaker on the unit, but it also has provision for an optional external horn that can be installed at a different location. This is a good option, and my own Owl has it. With the horn located near the ceiling or outside the room, apart from the sensor unit, intruders would find it less easy to deactivate the alarm.

A most effective and relatively inexpensive alarm system is this Owl Model 200 by Web Electronics. It is a proximity-type alarm, and will trip no matter how quietly an intruder moves.

of the average shooter or collector. Then, I discovered a nice little device that costs less than a hundred dollars, and it works perfectly.

It's made by Web Detection, Incorporated, 2000 Shames Drive, Westbury, New York 11590, and it's called the Owl, Model 200. It doesn't depend on sound, it's a proximity device, detecting any movement within 20 feet of its location. It operates on two 9-volt alkaline batteries, and a pair of these is provided with

The unit is turned on and off with a removable machine-cut key, and when you first turn it on, you have about 20 seconds to get clear. After that, anyone who comes in and moves around, no matter how silently, will trigger it in 10 seconds.

The siren on the unit is fairly loud, but the remote horn emits a piercing, ear-splitting shriek. It's easily heard through closed doors, downstairs to upstairs, and so on. The average intruder would probably start running at the first sound of it. If not, at least you'd be alerted. When I first tested the unit, my sons tried to outwit it by sneaking quietly past it. It triggered every time. On the rare occasions when every-one is to be away from the house, I turn on the Owl, figuring that even if it doesn't frighten the intruder away, my neighbor will hear it whooping and come to investigate—with a shotgun.

Evaluation and Insurance

Every gun owner, especially one who has sev-eral guns or a collection, should have a master list that contains a description and the serial number of each gun. The list should be dated, and should also show the current cash value of

When the guns are all modern sporting or de-fense types, your local gun shop will usually give a fair appraisal of replacement cost. Who-ever handles the evaluation—make it plain that the guns are not for sale. This will tend to pro-

Separate insurance on your handguns is always a good idea, and is imperative when your battery includes items such as this $1,300 Agner target pistol.

each piece. To obtain an evaluation, the very best way is to have a professional appraisal. If the guns are ever stolen, or if you should unex-pectedly go to the Big Range In The Sky, the appraiser's fee will have been money well spent. Most insurance companies will accept a professional appraisal in setting a figure for reimbursement—in fact, quite a few of the ap-praisals I've done have been *for* insurance com-panies.

tect you from the dishonest evaluator who might value a piece low, then try to buy it from you. At the other extreme is the appraiser who over-values the guns, in order to increase his fee. The only way to guard against this is to have some idea of the approximate value of your handguns, and know the reputation of your appraiser. I base my appraisal fees on three factors: The number of guns involved, the amount of re-search required, and total collection value.

Keep in mind that the value of any handgun depends on several important points: Condition, Scarcity, and Demand. These will apply whether the gun is a collector's piece or a practical-use firearm. In the practical-use department, a good used Colt Python or a Government Model pistol will bring a respectable price because many shooters want these guns. On the other hand, I've seen some rare handguns go for very low prices, because there's not much collector interest in them. Finally, remember that a single tiny marking in some obscure place on the handgun can often add many dollars to the collector value of a particular piece.

If you own only one gun, your regular homeowner's insurance might cover its loss. If you have several valuable pieces though, most policies require a separate rider listing them individually, at extra cost. If you're an NRA member, they have a good insurance plan for those who need to insure several guns. Most policies will also cover the possibility of fire damage. Firearms can be a valuable asset, in the same way as your home, vehicles, and other property—so, it's a good idea to protect your investment with insurance.

Gunsmithing

Over the years, I've seen a few excellent repair jobs that were done by talented amateurs. Without exception, these were done by experienced and knowledgeable shooters who also happened to be skilled with tools. On the other hand, I've seen hundreds of crude home-made parts, poorly-fitted factory replacement parts, and guns that were badly damaged by amateur repair attempts. So, I've arrived at the conclusion that in most cases, repairs should be left to a competent, professional gunsmith.

In some areas of the country, though, this last bit of advice is not easy to follow. In recent times, firearms repair has become divided into two categories, the Parts Replacer and the Specialist. When a part breaks in a modern handgun, the Parts Replacer is usually capable of disassembling the piece and installing a factory replacement for the broken part, but only in cases where no precise fitting is required. In many modern handguns, the generous tolerances allowed in manufacturing will work in his favor. I feel, though, that calling the Parts Replacer a Gunsmith is stretching the term.

At the other end of the scale is the Specialist, and he definitely deserves the title of Gunsmith or Pistolsmith. This category includes people like Behlert, Chow, Swenson, Clark, and other custom shops. Some of the work they turn out is absolutely beautiful. For the average shooter, though, there are some drawbacks in calling on a specialist for routine repair jobs. They are relatively—and, justifiably—expensive, and there's usually a long waiting period. Mainly, the problem is that most of them restrict their work to one or two particular handguns. If your handgun is a GM Colt, no problem; if it happens to be a SIG/Sauer P220, they won't touch it.

Even among the few general gunsmiths that are left, I've noticed that quite a few will refuse to do repair work on such things as old top-break revolvers. A part of this, I think, may be the liability thing, an uneasiness that some defect, even one unrelated to the work done, may cause some injury and a lawsuit. I've never subscribed to this idea, but I have frequently added warnings to repair bills about things like full-reach firing pins and safe carrying practices. Then, if something happens, I can show that they were warned.

When choosing a local gunsmith, the best guide a gun owner can use is reputation. A few ruined pieces will soon label the inept workman as a "gun butcher." It also works the other way, of course. The man who consistently turns out quality work will be known for this in his area. In a situation where there's no word-of-mouth recommendation, one alternative would be to try the gunsmith with a routine job on a less-important gun, to gauge his work. Then, you can decide whether to entrust him with your "jewel."

A handgun that has collector value is almost always worth repairing. In some cases, though, an older practical-use gun that is extremely worn and loose may prove to be beyond reclamation. For old American handguns and many pre-war foreign pieces, replacement parts are difficult or impossible to find. Anything that must be replaced will have to be made by the gunsmith. This can become expensive, and often the cost can exceed the value of the gun. Of course, if the old Forehand & Wadsworth was carried by the owner's grandfather as Sheriff of the County, that's another story.

Safety Rules

Before we leave the Care section of the book, a few end-notes on safety. As noted earlier, the original "Ten Commandments" are still quite valid for sport shooting, but they contain several conflicts when applied to the personal protection use of handguns. So, I'll propose my own set of Handgun Safety Rules, herewith:

1. Watch the muzzle direction! (This is the equivalent of Rules 1, 4, and 6 in the original ten.)

2. Check to see if the gun is loaded. Don't depend on the mechanism. Visually inspect the chamber(s).

3. Never leave a loaded handgun where it is accessible to children or inexperienced adults.

4. Be thoroughly familiar with all of the safety mechanisms of your handgun.

5. When shooting, keep in mind the range and penetration possibilities. Be sure of your backstop. (In home defense, remember that a wall will not necessarily stop a bullet. In the street, have concern for any innocent bystanders.)

6. When shooting, be sure your companions are well to the rear of your firing point. (With revolvers, there is always some escape of gas and powder grains at the cylinder/barrel gap. With autos, there is the ejection of fired cases.)

7. Be alert to the possibility of ricochets, from pavement, buildings, or water surfaces. (It should be noted that a bullet will ricochet from water only if fired at a very shallow angle.)

8. Carry your handgun safely, in a holster or case.

9. Use only ammunition in a power range recommended for your particular handgun.

10. Always remember that mechanical safety devices are not a substitute for safe handling practices.

Section Two

Gun Cleaning

ALMOST EVERYONE who has ever fired a handgun knows, of course, how to clean it. You just lock the slide open, or swing out the cylinder, and use a brush or a patch and some solvent to scrub out the chamber or chambers and the bore. Well, the method just described is better than no cleaning at all, but it will miss a lot of residue. It also raises a few questions, and some of the questions are those I've heard often. Which solvent is best? Which type of cleaning rod, and which tip? Which is best, a brush, or a patch? And especially, is it harmful to clean from the muzzle, rather than from the breech end?

Some of these are easily answered: There is no "best" solvent. There are several good ones, and certain types are best suited to certain cleaning jobs. We'll be looking at some of these, a little further on. Similar criteria apply to the cleaning rods, brushes, and patches. The other question, though, about cleaning from the muzzle, is not so easily answered. For example, it's obvious that with some handguns, such as re-volvers and muzzleloading single-shot pistols, cleaning from the muzzle is the only feasible way. And yet, serious target shooters know that a tiny nick or deformation of the rifling at the edge of the muzzle can affect accuracy. This would seem to be another of those insoluble problems, but it's not.

First of all, the actual hazards of from-the-muzzle cleaning have been exaggerated. Normal cleaning procedures, even when the rod used is of a fairly hard material like stainless steel, will not cause enough wear to really matter. It would be possible, of course, to handle the rod so roughly that a rifling land could be damaged at the muzzle edge. On the other hand, this could even be done when cleaning from the breech, especially if the treatment was rough enough to actually bend the cleaning rod. The obvious pre-vention method here is simple—just handle the cleaning operation with the same care you use in all other firearms operations.

Another means of preventing damage to the rifling at the muzzle is mechanical. In various

When cleaning from the muzzle is the only possible way, a brass muzzle protector like this will keep the rod from touching the rifling. The coned section allows use with a wide range of calibers.

forms, many makers of cleaning equipment now offer little conical guides with knurled collars, usually known as muzzle guards. These are available as separate accessories, but often are standard equipment on the better cleaning rods. In use, the conical tip of the guard fits into the bore at the muzzle, centering the rod and keeping it from touching the edges of the rifling. These muzzle guards work exactly as intended, and for any shooter who is concerned with wear or damage in this area, they are definitely recommended.

Another cleaning concern, and this one includes the entire bore, is the material used for cleaning rods. Rods have been made of regular steel, stainless steel, brass, aluminum, fiberglass, nylon, and, especially in the muzzleloaders, of wood. Some of the materials named above have also been used with a soft plastic coating. A few years ago, when fiberglass was first used, it appeared mostly in combination ramrod-cleaning rod form, for use with muzzleloading pistols. There was some concern, initially, about the possible abrasive qualities of the fiberglass, and its effect on the rifling. At the time, I ran a test of this theory, using an old cut-off section of barrel that had excellent rifling.

With a very sensitive Mitutoyo dial caliper, I measured the inside diameter, land-to-land, of the bore. Then, I ran a fiberglass rod through the bore a few thousand times, and finally chucked a piece of it into an electric drill, and let it chatter around in the bore at high RPM. The dial caliper was then used again, and showed no measureable difference. So much for the "abrasive fiberglass" theory.

There's another "worry" that should be mentioned, this one concerning any cleaning rod that has a "soft" surface. This would include fiberglass, nylon, aluminum, wood, and plastic coating. The idea was that these materials might pick up and retain small bits or slivers of steel from the bore during normal use. Then, these imbedded pieces of steel would themselves become damaging abrasives, cutting into the rifling lands. This is theoretically possible, but only in a strict set of circumstances. If the gun is of lesser quality, and the bore is not smoothly finished, there's a possibility that the land edges of the rifling might have some detachable slivers of steel. When this is the case, and a soft rod is used, it might produce the condition described above.

Then again, it might not. I've always felt that the material used for cleaning rods should be chosen for strength and other qualities, and that the supposed abrasive possibilities are so small that they are of no importance. I have cleaning rods in all of the materials mentioned, and use them frequently, often in handguns that are relatively valuable. I've had some of these guns for more than 35 years, and shoot them often. Surely, any damage would have showed up by now. Let's look at a few representative examples of separate rods and cleaning kits, just to have an idea of what's available.

Equipment

While we're talking about handguns here, many dismountable section-type rifle rods can easily double as handgun rods, when the threaded joining tips are the same size and thread as patches, a bronze brush, and a plastic jag-type patch tip.

A similar kit, but of higher quality and costing a bit more, stays in my range box. It's by

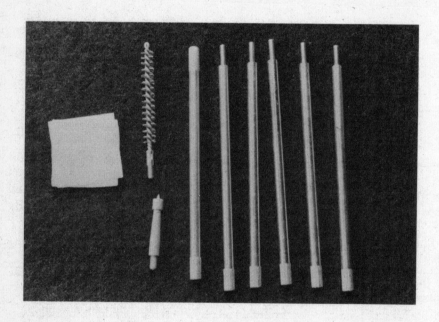

Tipco's Pac-Ram set has an aluminum sectioned rod that assembles to 32-inch length, and comes in different calibers. It takes down into a very small package, and is inexpensive.

the standard brushes, patch tips, and "mops." A neat and low-priced kit that I keep in the glove compartment of my truck is the Pac-Ram, made by Tipco Industries, 87 Main Street, Hastings-on-Hudson, New York 10706. It consists of a knurled-end handle-piece and five sections, all aluminum, each 5¼ inches long. This kit comes in a soft plastic roll-up case with a snap closure, and separate pockets for each rod section. A fold-in flap has pockets that hold

Outers, Box 39, Onalaska, Wisconsin 54650, one of the oldest and best names in gun cleaning equipment. This kit is called the Imperial Pak-Rod, and its alternate rifle-pistol use is noted on its soft plastic case. The sectioned rod here is of solid brass, and the head of the handle section is a nicely-knurled knob of ½-inch diameter. The five sections are each 6 inches long. In the flap pockets, there are a mop, a slotted nylon patch-tip, a bronze brush, and a "bore obstruction

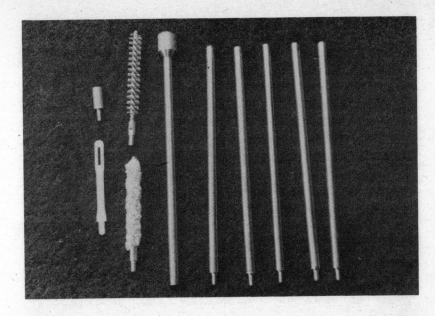

The Imperial Pak-Rod kit is solid brass, and of high quality. Because of the inclusion of a bronze brush, it comes in different calibers. The rod knob is nicely knurled.

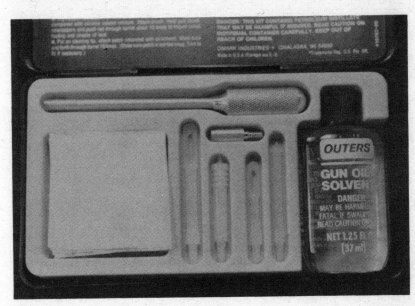

Strictly for "normal" handgun barrel lengths (up to 4½ inches), the Outers Field Kit contains all the items necessary for a quick clean-up at the range or in the outback.

tip." The last item named is a nice addition, a small cylinder of knurled brass with a concave end, perfect for pushing out a stuck bullet, a patch, or any other object in the bore.

You'll note that these two kits, made for specific caliber ranges, each contain a bronze brush. In kits that are designed to be used for all types of handguns and long guns, a brush is normally not included—these should be obtained by the user in the specific calibers needed. Be-

fore we leave the mini-kits, there's a particularly neat one by Outers that's intended for handguns having barrels of 4½ inches or less. It comes in a hard plastic case with a hinged lid, the case measuring just 5¾ by 3¾ by 1½ inches. Inside, in compartments, are a 3-inch aluminum rod with a 1¾-inch knurled handle of ½-inch diameter, and five accessory tips. These include a knurled aluminum adapter for brushes, and four slotted and jag-type patch tips, in two

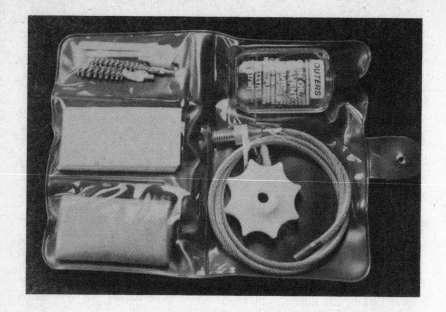

The Outers Pocket-Pak Kit has a flexible plastic-covered steel cable for a "rod," and is adaptable to both handgun and long-gun use.

The Universal Kit by Outers covers the cleaning of handguns, rifles, and shotguns. In addition to the cleaning hardware, it contains patches, solvent, and gun oil. The attractive and durable case is hard plastic.

sizes. There is also a stack of patches, and in a soft plastic bottle at the end is a combination gun oil and solvent solution. The rod turns freely in the handle, to allow the patch to follow the rifling.

Outers also offers a Pocket-Pak field cleaning kit that is no larger than the one above, but will accomodate longer barrels, and can even be used for rifles. Its "rod" is a flexible steel braided cable covered in soft plastic, and it's designed for pull-through operation. The large and comfortable plastic handle is screwed onto the cable endpiece, the cable is inserted through the bore, and a brush or patch is then attached and pulled through. This kit is in a fold-over soft plastic case with a snap closure and pockets for the items. Included are a bottle of the gun oil-solvent combination, patches, a silicone-treated cloth, and two brushes, two patch-tips, and an adapter.

A smaller version of the Universal Kit by Outers, this is the Pistol & Revolver Kit. Containing a bronze brush, it is purchased by caliber.

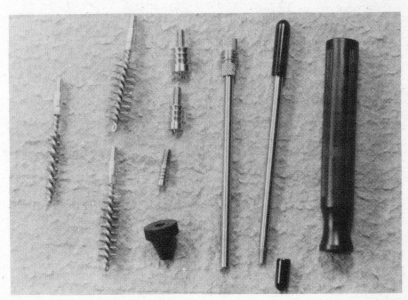

The RR8-2 Kit by RIG is a very compact unit that assembles into an 8-inch stainless-steel rod, and covers calibers from 22 to 45. It also includes a plastic muzzle guard.

The kits described above are fine for the range box or for in-the-field cleaning, but for the home base most shooters will want a more complete outfit. Outers has two good ones—a Universal kit for rifles, shotguns, and handguns, and a kit designed especially for pistols and revolvers. Both are in hard plastic boxes with removable lids and recesses for the items. The Universal kit has a three-section free-turning rod with a large plastic handle and a total assembled length of 30½ inches. There are patch tips for all three types of guns, and knurled brush adapters for each. The rod and the adapters are aluminum. Also included are a box of patches, and separate bottles of gun oil and solvent.

The handgun kit also has the oil, solvent, and patches, and a single-section rod, 7½ inches long. Included are slotted and jag-type patch tips, a mop, and a bronze brush. Both of these kits by Outers are excellent for the shooter who

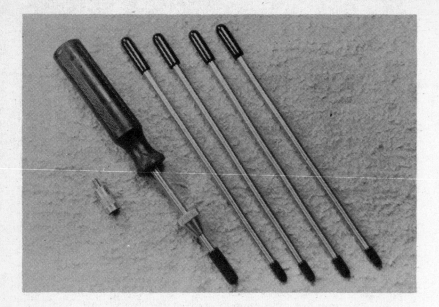

The standard RIG-Rod has a sectioned stainless-steel shaft that assembles to 31½ inches, and is usable for any handgun barrel and for long guns as well. Included are a brass muzzle guard and an adapter for shotgun fittings.

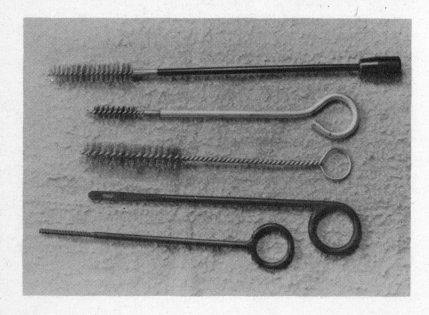

Here are examples of factory-supplied cleaning implements by Benelli, Smith & Wesson, Beretta, and Walther.

wants all of the necessary items in one package. For those who prefer to assemble their own cleaning outfits, the most important item is a good cleaning rod. In the easily-carried takedown type, one of the best is the RIG-Rod, by RIG Products, 87 Coney Island Drive, Sparks, Nevada 89431. This stainless steel rod has every good feature a cleaning rod could have. The large plastic handle has a 3½-inch free-turning section, and there are four 7-inch rod sections.

For storage, all of the attachment ends are neatly encased in plastic caps. A conical brass muzzle-guard with a knurled collar is included, along with an adapter for shotgun accessories. This rod can be used for handguns, rifles, or shotguns, and the user can pick his own accessories. RIG also has a fine two-part handgun rod for 2- to 7½-inch barrels, in their kit #RR8-2. In addition to the handle and the two rod sections there are three patch jags and three bronze brushes in

The gas-locked Steyr GB pistol comes with a particularly fine set of cleaning equipment. There are bronze and stainless steel brushes for the bore and the gas cylinder, a slotted patch tip, and a very well-made rod with a ball handle.

22, 38, and 45 calibers, and a conical plastic muzzle protector.

Now let's consider the one-piece, non-takedown handgun rods. Anyone who has ever bought a new, in-the-box revolver or pistol has probably received a cleaning rod or a twisted-wire-handle brush, at no extra cost. It's rare to find a new handgun that doesn't have one of these as standard equipment. In these factory-supplied implements, there's a wide range of quality and utility. Most of the small European automatics that were imported prior to 1968 had a fiber brush with a twisted-wire handle, and while this was better than nothing, it wasn't adequate for a really thorough cleaning.

Some more modern examples, in the larger guns, show items that are really useful. Smith & Wesson has, at various times, included an aluminum rod with a loop handle, and a bronze brush attachment or a mop, sometimes both. I can remember that a new S&W 22 Kit Gun that I traded for around 1958 had all three pieces. In the automatics, my Walther PP-Super has a nice loop-handle rod with a slotted patch-tip that's made of nylon or some tough plastic. The Benelli B76 has a well-made rod of black-anodized aluminum with a plastic knob, fitted with a good-quality replaceable bronze brush.

Some factory cleaning equipment is even more complete. My Steyr GB pistol has a black aluminum rod with a smooth plastic ball knob, a slotted nylon patch tip with a steel screw attachment, and two brushes, one bronze and the other stainless steel. The smaller-diameter bronze brush is for the bore, and the larger stainless steel brush is for cleaning the gas cylinder of this gas-locked pistol. These brushes are also notable for having a very fine feature, screw-attachments at both ends. Thus, when the bristles "lay back" after long use, the brush can be reversed. The quality of all these items is superb. If all of the gun makers began to follow the example of Steyr, the manufacturers of cleaning equipment would soon be in trouble. This is not going to happen, so there will always be a market for quality rods and other accessories. One good example of a quality one-piece rod is the one made by Parker-Hale of England, and sold in the U.S. by Freeland's, 3737 14th Avenue, Rock Island, Illinois 61201. I have a 22 caliber Parker-Hale rod that has an 8-inch shaft of plastic-coated steel, revolving freely in a comfortably-shaped plastic handle. This rod comes with a 3-inch screw-on jag tip for patches, but I also have a bronze brush, a nylon brush, and a mop attachment for it. All of the

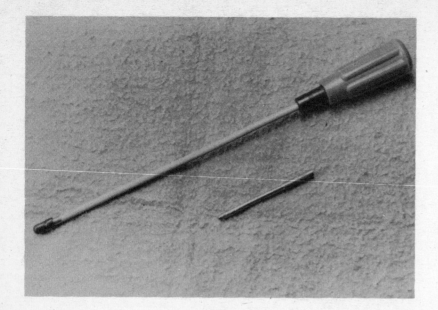

A 22-caliber example of the fine Parker Hale handgun rod. The shaft is plastic-covered, and a jag-type patch tip is shown. Many other fittings are available.

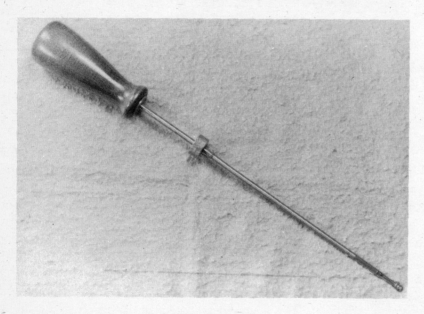

This high-quality rod by Durango has a brass muzzle guard, and is shown with a jag-type patch tip attached.

Parker-Hale items are of excellent quality.

There's a fine 9-inch stainless steel rod that I've been using for several years, made by Durango, U.S.A., Incorporated of Durango, Colorado 81301. It has a large hardwood handle, an integral brass muzzle guard, and the rod is free-turning. The end of the rod has a threaded tip, and an adapter sleeve, which allows the use of male or female attachments. With the sleeve and a jag patch tip in place, total length of the rod portion is 10 3/4 inches, long enough for any handgun with a barrel of 8 inches or less. I haven't seen one of these rods for a while, but if the company is still in business, it's a very good one.

Uncle Mike's—Michaels of Oregon, Box 13010, Portland, Oregon 97213—makes a strong and nicely-made fixed-shaft rod of stainless steel for calibers of 357 and larger. It's their #2829, made as a muzzle-loading accessory, to

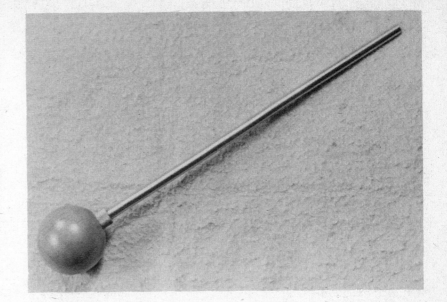

By Uncle Mike's—Michaels of Oregon—this non-rotating stainless steel rod has a large ball-type knob, and was designed to double as a loading rod for muzzle-loaders. It is very nicely made.

To accommodate even the long-barreled handguns of the silhouette game, Outers makes a 10-inch brass and a 20-inch stainless rod, both with large and comfortable handles.

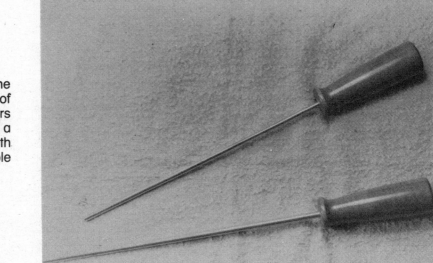

double as a ramrod, but I've used it often as a general cleaning rod. The heavy 10-inch rod screws into a knurled brass fitting set into a large round knob of smooth wood. The end of the rod is internally threaded 10-32, to work with Michaels #2901 accessory kit, as well as with some others. To work with Outers and Hoppe's accessories, there's an adapter available, #2906.

In recent months, I've been trying two excel-lent rods by Outers, their Imperial #40333 and #40336 rods. The first is a 10-inch rod of brass with a large and comfortable wooden handle and a free-turning shaft. It's slim enough to handle 22 caliber, and strong enough for anything up to 45 caliber. The other rod, #40336, is of the same design, but has a 20-inch shaft of stainless steel. Of larger diameter, it will handle any bore from 30 caliber upward. This one is particularly useful on the longer-barreled guns used in Sil-

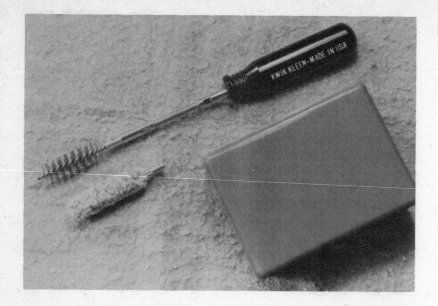

The Kwik-Kleen kit, with its flexible shaft, is made for cleaning chambers without field-stripping the gun. In an emergency, it could also be used to clean the entire bore of a short barrel. The handle, shaft, bronze brush, and mop fit into the small plastic case shown.

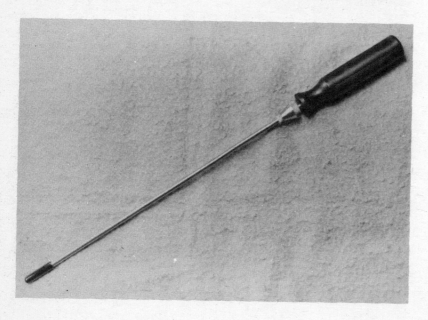

RIG has an excellent 11-inch rod that is long enough for everything but the Silueta handguns. It comes with a brass muzzle guard.

houette match shooting. I use it often on my Martz Luger Carbine, which has a 12-inch barrel. Both of these rods are internally threaded at the end for all Outers accessories, and they come in heavy clear plastic tubes for convenient storage.

Another interesting "rod" is the Kwik-Kleen, designed for chambers only. While its main application is for removing plastic shell residue from shotgun chambers without disassembly, it can also be used in automatic pistols, and the company offers a Kwik-Kleen unit for this purpose. When a lot of firing is done, as in match shooting, reliability is enhanced by occasional cleaning of just the chamber. This unit will do this without the necessity of field-stripping. It consists of a plastic handle that attaches to a short length of flexible spring-cable. The tip of the cable is internally threaded to accept Outers brushes and mops. The flexibility allows inser-

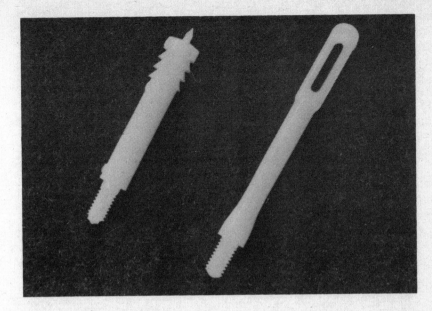

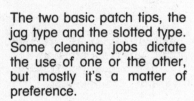

The two basic patch tips, the jag type and the slotted type. Some cleaning jobs dictate the use of one or the other, but mostly it's a matter of preference.

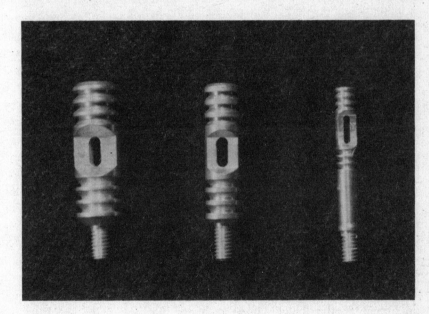

The Two-Way Tip from Ox-Yoke Originals combines the features of the jag tip and the slotted tip. It keeps the patch in contact with the rifling on both the inward and outward strokes.

tion of the brush or mop into the chamber through the ejection port, with the slide locked open. For more information and current prices, the address is: Kwik-Kleen Company, Inc., Box 9764, Yakima, Washington 98909.

Among the fine rods by RIG Products is an 11-inch free-turning rod of stainless steel that has a comfortable plastic handle and comes with a brass conical muzzle protector. This one is supplied in a nice hard-plastic storage tube, and like all of the RIG rods, it has a slip-on cap of soft plastic to protect its internally-threaded end. The shaft is of 3/16-inch diameter, so this rod can be used in calibers from 22 upward. For use with this rod, RIG offers patch jags and loop-type patch tips in three sizes, to cover all calibers from 22 to 45.

There are, of course, other good cleaning rods—the ones described are just a sampling. With available adapters, most can be used with

The round patches on the right are Hoppe's Reemay, and the others are from Outers and Brownells. The latter two are cotton flannel.

almost any accessories. Let's look at some of these, and their intended uses: Patch tips are of two basic types—slotted, and jag. The jag types are made in many forms, but all have some sort of flanges or projections to hold a wrapped patch. This type has to be used in single-shot muzzle-loaders, but many shooters prefer the jag tip for cleaning cartridge handguns, because saturated used patches can be conveniently shaken off the tip into a wastebasket.

On the other hand, a slotted tip will hold the patch for a repeated run-through of the bore. Each has its advantages, so it's a matter of individual choice. A recent innovation by Ox-Yoke Originals, 130 Griffin Road, Suffield, Connecticut 06093, is a Two-Way Tip, a brass rod attachment that has patch jags at each end, and a slot at the middle. The jag flutes are angled toward the center, to grip the patch on both the inward and outward strokes. It works just as they claim, and does a good job. "Two-Way Tip" is a registered trade mark, and a patent has been applied for.

Patch material seems to have been pretty well standardized, a soft flannel with one side "fuzzy" and the other neutral, but there have been some variations. I have some Hoppe's patches made of Reemay, a Du Pont product that has good bore-scrubbing properties, and they work well. Reemay is composed of continuous-filament polyester fibers that are bonded together to make a lint-free material with tiny loops and coils to catch and hold particles of residue. Another advantage is that solvents and oils are not absorbed, but are held in this latticework for dispersal. For those who prefer the traditional cotton flannel patch, Brownells, Route Two, Box One, Montezuma, Iowa 50171, offers these in bulk packs of a thousand, in four sizes.

In shape, patches are square, round, or rectangular, and are sized according to caliber. Sometimes, depending on the rod tip used, even a patch of the right size will fit the bore too tightly. When this happens, you can just trim the patch until it's a snug but free-moving fit. Round patches generally work best with jag-type tips, and square or rectangular ones with slotted tips. In addition to the unique patch tip described above, Ox-Yoke Originals also offers a square synthetic patch that has two opposed cuts, almost to the center. When inserted into the Two-Way Tip the flared "wings" of the patch lay back evenly, giving more bore contact area and a better fit. I have also tried this superior patch in regular slotted tips, and it works well in them, too, but it's best when used with

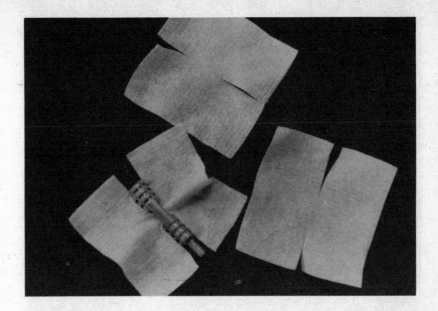

These unusually-cut patches are made by Ox-Yoke especially for the Two-Way Tip. The twin cuts allow the patch to "lay back" along the jag portions of the tip.

Examples of handgun-sized "mop" attachments. These are best used for after-cleaning oil application.

their specially designed Two-Way Tip.

Used and soiled patches are meant to be thrown away, but mop attachments are not, and if used for cleaning they will soon be ruined. Mops are best reserved for the after-cleaning application of oil or some other preservative agent. They will do this better than a patch, because their long contact area and great absorbency will distribute the lubricant more completely and evenly. I don't know whether this was the

original idea for these mops, but it's certainly the best use of them.

Most of the non-metallic bore brushes have bristles of either fiber or nylon, and these are fine for removing loose powder grains and similar residue. For hard scale or metal deposits, though, they are not effective. These require a good stainless steel or bronze brush. Of these two, the stainless steel will get deposits that even a good bronze brush will miss. Stainless

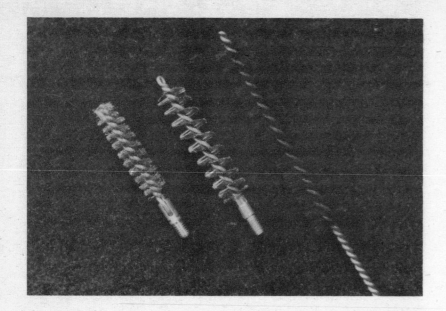

Cleaning brushes and brush attachments generally are made of bronze, stainless steel, or fiber. Nylon has also been used for some brushes.

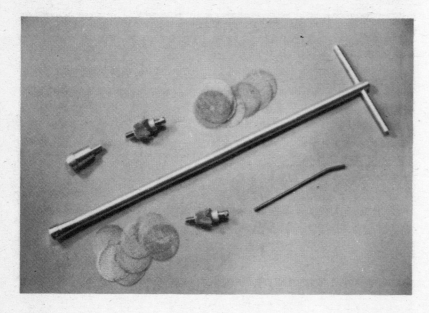

The Lewis Lead Remover consists of T-handle rod and two end-pieces. One is a cone-shaped fitting for use in the forcing cone of revolvers, and the other is a compressible rubber piece for cylinder chambers and auto pistol barrels. They are used with "brass cloth" patches. Fittings are offered in three sizes, to cover calibers from 38 to 45.

steel bristles retain more spring for a longer time than bronze, which will eventually take a set and lie down. Most of the makers of cleaning accessories now offer brushes in stainless steel in all sizes. I still use bronze brushes for some jobs, but in time I'll probably use stainless exclusively.

Those who do a lot of shooting with cast lead or lead alloy bullets will inevitably have some problems with lead deposits in the bore. If the loads are near magnum-level, the problem will be more pronounced, as the higher velocities will tend to increase the lead transfer. With a good brush, some solvent, and a lot of scrubbing, you can usually remove light deposits. When the accumulation is really heavy, though, a specialized tool is needed: This is the Lewis Lead Remover, made by L. E. M. Gun Specialties, Incorporated, Box 31, College Park, Georgia 30337.

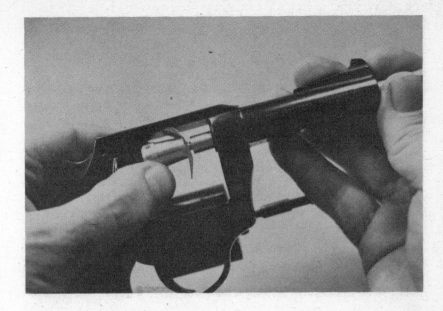

With the cylinder swung out, the rod is inserted from the muzzle, and the conical tip and brass patch are attached to the end of the rod. The tips are cross-drilled, and a pin-wrench is provided for tightening.

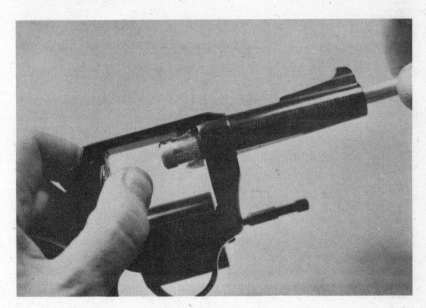

Holding the gun firmly, in the hand or a padded vise, the conical tip and patch are pulled forward into the barrel cone and given a right-hand rotation. With heavy leading, it may be necessary to back out the patch and knock off the lead flakes, then repeat the operation.

The Lewis tool consists of an aluminum rod with a T-handle and two attachments. One is a solid cone-shaped piece for use in the forcing cone of revolver barrels, and the other has a compressible rubber section, for use in revolver cylinder chambers and automatic pistol barrels. There are attachments in three different sizes, to work in 38, 41, and 44 or 45 calibers. These fittings are used with "patches" of brass mesh which are sized to the corresponding caliber.

To remove lead from the forcing cone, the rod is inserted from the muzzle, and the cone-shaped piece, with a brass "patch" attached, is screwed onto the rod tip. The piece is then pulled tight against the forcing cone and turned to remove the lead. The compressible rubber piece is used in much the same way. There is a cross-hole in the shank of the rubber piece for insertion of a pin-wrench to expand the rubber for proper patch contact. It should be a snug fit,

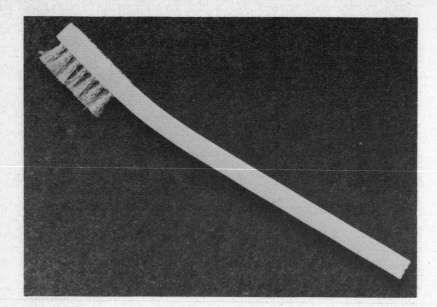

The most-used cleaning tool in my shop is this little stainless-steel brush from Brownells. For removal of surface lead and powder residue, it is absolutely indispensible.

but not too tight, or the brass patch may strip off. There is nothing else like the Lewis Lead Remover, and nothing will work as well to remove lead from the forcing cone of a revolver.

There are areas to be cleaned on pistols and revolvers where a round brush is practically useless. The round brush, in addition to its use in the chamber and bore, is also perfect for the feed ramp and magazine well of automatic pistols, but on any flat or convex surface it doesn't have enough contact surface to do the job. For these, you need a toothbrush shape. In fact, a regular toothbrush is excellent, if it has fairly stiff bristles and you're dealing with ordinary powder residue. Unfortunately, most toothbrushes that are used for this purpose are discarded ones, with turned-over bristles. A new brush, bought for this purpose, is better.

When it's powder scale, the baked-on residue that accumulates around the barrel/cylinder gap in revolvers, then a brush with more authority is needed. This also applies to automatic pistols, especially those with gas systems, such as the Heckler & Koch P7. Brownells, the great gunsmith supply source, has an excellent toothbrush-shaped stainless steel brush that I've been using for years. It has good stiff stainless bristles, and perfect dimensions. Its catalog number

is 4D00PLL, and the address is Brownells, Incorporated, Route Two, Box One, Montezuma, Iowa 50171. I have not found a better brush, and I use one of these in every cleaning job. Every serious shooter should have one on hand.

Even with the best brushes, there will be some areas that can't be reached, and should be cleaned. Some examples are the extractor and ejector slots in automatic pistols, and the area above the rear protrusion of the barrel in revolvers. For deep and narrow spaces like these, there is one best implement: The dental tool. These are made in an almost infinite variety of shapes, are usually made of stainless steel, and have knurled handles. The ones that I use were mostly obtained from dentists who had retired them because of broken tips. These were easily recut to give sharp points or other shapes, as needed. If your dentist doesn't have any discards, Brownells offers a set of useful shapes, stock number 2T00DES, and the cost is moderate.

As any user of factory lead or home-cast bullets will know, the inevitable build-up of deposited lead at the step of the chamber is difficult to remove. When the step is fairly sharp and pronounced, even the Lewis tool can't get all of the deposit. For this you need the Clymer cylinder de-leading tool. This is a precision-ground cut-

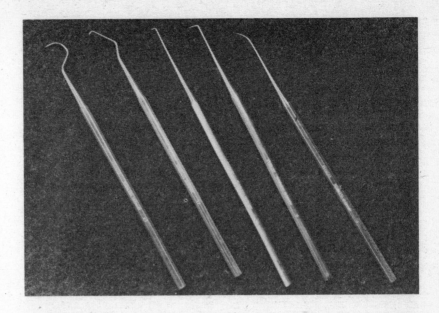

This dental tool set from Brownells contains five shapes that are very useful for removing residue from small recesses. The tools are made of stainless steel.

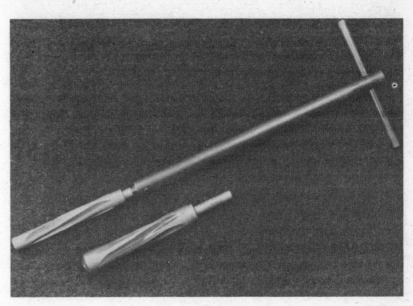

This precision tool set by Clymer is for removing lead from the chamber steps in revolvers. The 38/357 and 44 reamers are shown.

ting tool that is similar to the famous Clymer reamers, but carefully designed to cut only lead, up to the step. It's sized .0005-inch smaller than the SAAMI minimum chamber specifications, and is available in 38/357, 41, 44, and 45 calibers. Made of high-speed steel and hardened to 62/64 on the Rockwell C scale, these de-leading tools should last practically forever. They're used with hand power only, and a T-handle is available from Clymer to hold the tools for turn-

ing. Their five flutes prevent chatter, and they really do a fine job. I use the 357 and 44 tools often. The address is Clymer Manufacturing Company, 14241 West Eleven Mile Road, Oak Park, Michigan 48237.

When a barrel is entirely removable, as in many automatic pistols, or when the breech end is accessible for a straight-through view, inspecting the bore is a simple matter. With the barrel aimed toward a light source or a well-lit

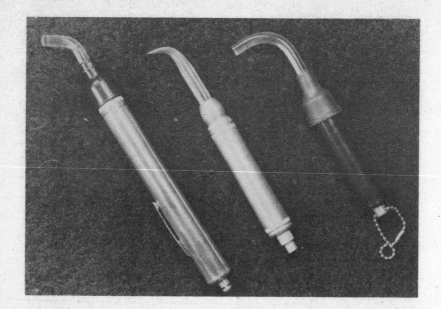

Most bore-lights follow a familiar pattern, using either one or two AA-cell batteries and a curved Lucite endpiece. Some typical examples are shown.

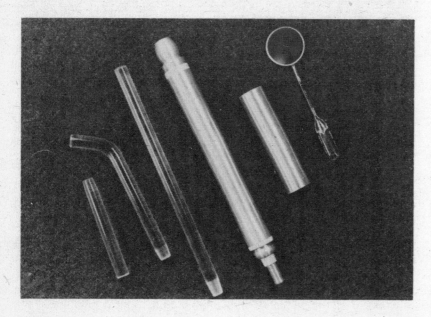

The ultimate bore-light of this type is Brownells Conduct-A-Lite. It comes with three different Lucite extensions, a shorter body piece for one-cell operation, and a clip-on mirror.

white surface, a visual inspection of the bore is easy. For a look without takedown, and for revolvers, some type of accessory is needed. Reflecting devices are available, some with angled mirrors, but these are sometimes less than satisfactory. They depend on an exact angle in relation to the bore and the outside light source, and the illumination they provide is uneven and often too bright in spots.

A battery-powered bore-light is much better, and there are many types. The minimum bore-light is just a regular push-button penlight with the addition of a curved lucite endpiece that "bends" the light into the chamber or bore. Perhaps the ultimate version of this type is the Conduct-A-Lite kit marketed by Brownells. It's made of aluminum, and uses two penlight batteries. It comes in a soft plastic pocket case that contains the light, an extra short body for single battery use, three lucite rods of various shapes

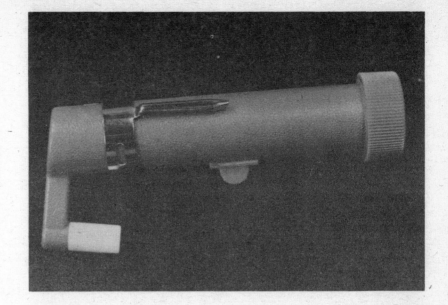

A bore-light that I use a lot is this Flashette. It has a translucent bulb cover that gives a soft light, and a positive switch. The light source is at exactly the right angle.

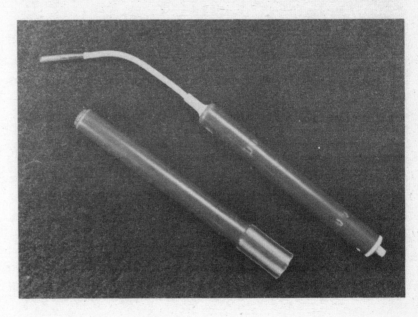

From a maker of medical tools, this MDS Probe-Lite has a tiny bulb and a shaft that can be bent into any shape. It has a positive toggle switch, and its batteries are replaceable. It supplies an intense light.

and lengths, a dental-type mirror that will clip onto the rods, and a spare bulb. You add the batteries, of course. It's a good outfit, and Brownells stock number is 7B10N87.

Another light that I use frequently is the "Flashette." This is a two-cell light made of sturdy ABS Acrylic plastic, and it uses a sub-miniature screw-in bulb. This light has two advantages, one of which is a translucent white bulb cover that gives a bright but soft non-glare light. The other plus is its fixed extension arm which places the bulb in line with the bore. Also, there's a sliding switch on the side, so you don't have to hold down a button during its use. This light is well-engineered from a convenient-use standpoint, and it's very inexpensive. The maker is the Flashette Company, 4725 South Kolin Avenue, Chicago, Illinois 60632.

The lights of the type described above are fine for a general through-view of the bore, but there

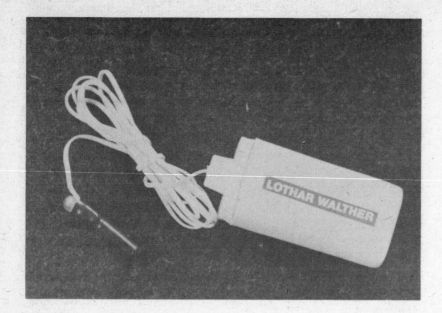

By Lothar Walther of West Germany, this tiny light has a weighted base and a long cord. It is for inspection of muzzleloader barrels, and uses two AA-type batteries.

are times when a lot of light may be needed on a specific spot, or in some recess of the handgun other than the bore. There's a light for this, too, and it's made by MDS Incorporated, Box 1441, Brandon, Florida 34299. The "MDS" in the company name stands for Medical Diagnostic Services, and the Probe-Lite had its beginning as a piece of medical equipment. Its 1/8-inch diameter extension can be bent into any useful angle, and the tiny bulb can even be inserted into a 22 bore. The Probe-Lite is available with extensions of either 5- or 10-inch length, the latter costing slightly more. The light has a positive toggle-type switch, and both the batteries and the tiny bulb are replaceable.

Until recently, the only way shooters of sin-gle-shot muzzle-loading pistols could examine the bore was to remove the breech plug, a major undertaking. Now, Gremmel Enterprises, 271 Sterling Drive, Eugene, Oregon 97404, imports a marvelous little light by Lothar Walther of West Germany that allows a full view of any bore of 8mm (.315″) or larger. Using one of the tiny bulbs, this one frosted to prevent glare, the light has a 42-inch flexible cord and a steel weight under the bulb. The weight and the bulb base are encased in soft plastic. Obviously, with the long cord, this unit can also be used in muzzle-loading rifles. In use, the cord is plugged into the two-battery case, and the tiny light is just dropped down the bore. It works beautifully, and it's not expensive.

Solvents and Lubricants

To anyone who appreciates fine handguns, the swirl of clean-edged rifling in a mirror-polished bore is a thing of beauty. When this pretty mechanical picture also delivers accuracy, a steady hold is all that's necessary for perfect scores on the target range. It's a myth, though, that only a beautiful bore can provide accurate delivery of the bullet. I have a Model 1923 Commercial Luger that will consistently group into 2 inches and less at 25 yards, and its bore looks like 5 miles of bad road. The rifling is still prominent, and that's what counts. From this, you might imagine that a bright, smooth bore doesn't matter. Not so.

If I fired cast-bullet handloads through that rough bore, I'd quickly have a serious problem with lead deposits, intensified by the relatively high velocity of the 30 caliber Luger cartridge. Even when factory loads or full-jacketed reloads are used, the bore soon has quite a copper-nickel coating. In any bore, even a bright or smooth one, lead or copper deposits do occur. A rough bore just makes removal more difficult.

In the case of very heavy lead deposits, it may be necessary to use the Lewis Lead Remover on the bore, as previously described. For lighter deposits in an un-pitted bore, scrubbing with a bronze or stainless steel brush will often flick out an impressive shower of tiny lead flakes, but this won't get it all. As for the copper, a brush will just polish it. The only thing that will remove it is a good solvent. The first to come to mind is the venerable Hoppe's Number Nine. It comes in containers ranging in size from a 2-ounce bottle to a 1-gallon drum, and there is also a handy aerosol can.

Good old Hoppe's Number Nine does a fine job, loosening the lead and chemically attacking the copper deposits without harming the bore. There is one caution, though, that should be remembered when using Hoppe's Number Nine, and this also applies to most any metal-affecting solvent: The solution should not be left in long contact with plating, especially nickel. Just as it breaks down the copper deposits in the bore, it will also attack the surface of the nickel plating. Short-term contact during cleaning will normally do no harm, but afterward all traces of the solution should be removed from the surface.

Sinclair, International, 1200 Asbury Drive, New Haven, Indiana 46774, markets several cleaning agents, and they cater especially to the benchrest and metallic silhouette shooter. Since those who participate in these sports are always trying for the smallest possible group and the legendary pinpoint accuracy, perhaps we should look at some of the items they use. One of these is Marksmans Choice Bore Cleaner. I've tried

Perhaps the most familiar of all cleaning solvents, Hoppe's Number Nine has been around for a long time.

it, and it's very effective at removing powder residue, lead, and copper deposits. It should be used as a bore cleaner *only,* and with some caution. It will do bad things to any wood finish, and is harmful to most plastics. The nickel plate warning also applies here—wipe it off completely, and as soon as possible. Marksmans Choice (and no, it's not "Marksman's") is relatively expensive in comparison to other solvents, but it does do a fine job.

Another well-known solvent, especially among target shooters, is Marksmans Choice No. 7.

Actually designed for use on small engines, Quicksilver does a fine job on firearms.

Sinclair also markets other specialized cleaners, such as the Australian-made Sweet's 7.62 Solvent, designed specifically for copper removal, and Plumbex from West Germany, which has the same purpose. Sweet's 7.62 is a liquid, and Plumbex is in gel form. I haven't tried either of these, but I've heard good reports on both. One item that is marketed by Sinclair that I have tried is Quicksilver. It's actually not designed to be a gun item—it's an engine clean-

er, and someone discovered that it also works well as a powder solvent. Since it will remove carbon from spark plugs in a running engine, you can imagine how it treats powder residue.

For more than 25 years, Jim Brobst has been making his J-B bore cleaning compound, and so far he has sold more than a half-million little 2-ounce plastic jars of the stuff. Many top marksmen swear by it, but until recently, I hadn't tried it. Now that I have, I can under-

In paste form, J-B Bore Cleaning Compound is non-imbedding and very effective on metal deposits.

Birchwood Casey's Nitro Solvent comes in several forms. This is the 4½-ounce liquid container.

stand why it's so popular. It's in paste form, and this has some convenience advantages over liquids. J-B bore cleaner is intended for use with patches only, and when used according to the instructions it is very effective in the removal of metal deposits and powder residue. One of its properties that is stressed by the manufacturer is that it is "non-embedding"—it can easily be cleaned out of the bore with a dry patch. It should be noted that this is a compound, and if it's left unused for an extended time, its elements will tend to separate. In that case, it should be stirred before use. It is not expensive, and it does an excellent job. It's available from Jim Brobst, 299 Poplar Street, Hamburg, Pennsylvania 19526.

The Birchwood Casey Division of Birchwood Laboratories, 7900 Fuller Road, Eden Prairie, Minnesota 55344, makes products that cover the entire subject matter of this book, including refinishing. In this section, though, we're looking at solvents and lubricants. Birchwood Casey offers a fine Nitro Powder Solvent that also contains a rust inhibitor. For general cleaning of

actions, I use it frequently.

Outers has an excellent Nitro Solvent that removes lead and copper deposits and powder residue. One of its ingredients is acetone, so it shouldn't be allowed to come in contact with the finish of wood grips, and it will also attack some plastics. I mention this because of the extensive use of this material in modern handguns, such as the Heckler & Koch P9S and the Interdynamic KG-99. This does not mean that

Nitro Solvent by Outers is available in regular liquid and in an aerosol can, as shown. A combination Oil/Solvent is also included in several of the Outers cleaning kits.

G96 Solvent has an added ingredient that removes plastic residue, an important factor for those who have shotshell-chambered handguns.

Outers solvent shouldn't be used on guns of this type. Just avoid letting any extensive overflow from having long contact with the plastic parts. Outers solvent is available in regular liquid form and in spray cans.

G96 Nitro Solvent by Jet-Aer Corporation, Paterson, New Jersey 07524, is another good cleaner, and like most of this company's products, it comes in an aerosol spray can. One of its properties is an ingredient that will neutralize

the corrosive acid residue left in the chamber by plastic shotshells. This point may not be of interest to most handgun shooters, but it will have some importance to those who have the Thompson/Center Contender pistol with a barrel that will take the 410 shotshell.

This is just a sampling—there are other good solvents, some in regular liquid and some in aerosol spray cans. A few, like Hoppe's Number Nine, are offered in both forms. The aerosol

Gun Scrubber by Birchwood Casey is one of the best of the de-greasers. I use it frequently in my shop.

Another de-greaser, of more recent introduction, is RIG 3. It does an excellent job.

spray form has two advantages. I've seen shooters plunge brushes and patches directly into solvent bottles, and after this has been done several times, with a brush, the solution is contaminated with powder residue and other fouling, losing its effectiveness. There is also some loss of the more volatile ingredients from an opened solvent bottle, through evaporation. Another advantage is that the solvent can be sprayed directly into areas of the mechanism that are not

readily accessible to a patch or brush. Several aerosols have a slim plastic tube that attaches to the spray button for precise application.

Up to this point, we've been considering solvents that are intended primarily for cleaning the bore of a handgun, and the chamber or chambers. There are other areas to be considered, such as the breech face in revolvers and the ramp area in automatics. Most of the solvents mentioned will also do a creditable job here, but

As noted on the label of this G96 de-greaser, one of its uses is for removing oil from steel surfaces before applying cold chemical blue.

The Outers de-greaser is called Crud Cutter. Like the others, it removes all oil and residue, and dries quickly.

there are two other products that I use often which will do this even better: Birchwood Casey's Gun Scrubber, and Mitann's RIG 3. Both are classified as de-greasers as well as general cleaners, and some of the other makers have products that are similar.

Jet-Aer, for example, has a G96 item called Spray Gun De-Greaser, that's intended as a before-reblue treatment. Any of the de-greasers work well, though, at flushing powder residue and dirt out of internal mechanisms. I find them particularly useful for an operation that fits their generic name, removing excess oil from actions. Outers version of this stuff is called Crud Cutter, and I have recently been using it as often as the other two named earlier. It does a fine job.

All of the de-greasers evaporate quickly after use, leaving a clean, dry surface. Most of them have the small insert tube that attaches to the spray button for precise application. Most of them contain 1,1,1-Trichloroethane and other halogenated solvents, so you must heed the cautions on the labels about using them with adequate ventilation. Extensive contact with your skin is also a thing to be avoided. Used with the proper care, though, they are quite safe, and there is nothing else that will do the job as well.

Black-Solve and Fort Greene Ville's Buffalo Spit are two blackpowder solvents that are designed to be mixed with water.

chemical properties break down the residue more efficiently.

All of the major makers of firearms cleaning agents make special blackpowder products, and there are several solutions made in smaller quantity by suppliers of other muzzle-loading supplies. Since I have a long-running magazine column called "The Powder Horn" (now appearing in *Gun World*), I've tried all of them. They all work, some with more efficiency than others. Some, that is, do the job more quickly. I should point out that some of the products mentioned below may or may not be still in production, as my use of them dates, in some cases, to 10 years ago.

One of the oldest and perhaps the best known among the muzzle-loading fraternity is Black-Solve, made by the Chopie Manufacturing Company, 531 Copeland Avenue, La Crosse, Wisconsin 54601. It's a concentrate, with a small bottle making a quart when mixed with water. Another concentrated solvent, called Buffalo Spit, is offered by Fort Greene Ville Trading Company, 2 Front Drive, Little Hocking, Ohio 45742. It comes in a 16-ounce bottle with only about 1½ inches of solution in the bottom. The idea is to fill the remainder of the bottle with water, then mix the solution. Quite a few blackpowder shooters prefer these mix-it-yourself solvents, and they do work well.

Most blackpowder solvents are also recommended by their makers as patch lubricants. The idea, obviously, is to "clean while you shoot," and to some extent it does work this way. When a solvent is used as a patch lubricant, rather than saliva or grease, it reduces the amount of fouling and makes easier the loading of subsequent shots. With this use in mind, several makers have offered their blackpowder solvents in soft plastic squeeze-type bottles with flip-up applicator spouts in their caps.

Thompson/Center Arms, Farmington Road, Rochester, New Hampshire 03867, is deservedly famous for fine firearms. They also offer their Number Thirteen solvent and patch lubricant. The Hodgdon Powder Company, 6231 Robin-

As those who shoot muzzle-loading handguns know, the cleaning of blackpowder residue requires special solutions and procedures. Left in the bore and on other surfaces, the remains of blackpowder will quickly form salts that are very corrosive. In some climatic conditions, this can ruin a gun overnight. A good job of blackpowder cleaning can be done in the old fashion, with soap and hot water, but the modern solutions will do it better, and more easily. Their

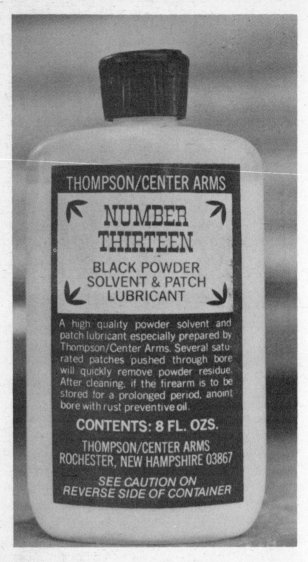

Thompson/Center's Number Thirteen, like several of the blackpowder solvents, is recommended as both a cleaner and patch lubricant.

Spit Bath, by Hodgdon Powder Company, is their blackpowder solvent. Their patch lubricant is a different solution, called Spit Ball.

son, Shawnee Mission, Kansas 66201, separates its related products into Spit Patch and Spit Bath, the latter being the true cleaning solvent. Hoppe's special blackpowder solvent is called Hoppe's 9 Plus. Many muzzle-loading shooters who also regularly use cartridge handguns, and who were already familiar with the regular Number Nine solvent, have naturally chosen 9 Plus for their blackpowder handguns.

In the same way, the cartridge handgunners

who were Birchwood Casey fans moved to Number 77 Black Powder Solvent when they became interested in muzzle-loading handguns. Birchwood Casey Number 77 also has some popularity among non-muzzle-loading target shooters. Actually, there's no reason that any of the specialized blackpowder solvents couldn't be used to clean smokeless-powder cartridge guns. The only drawback might be that they often do not have the copper-removing ingredi-

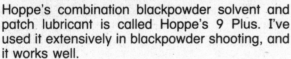

Hoppe's combination blackpowder solvent and patch lubricant is called Hoppe's 9 Plus. I've used it extensively in blackpowder shooting, and it works well.

Another popular blackpowder solvent is Birchwood Casey Number 77. In addition to its use by the muzzleloaders, it is also liked by target shooters.

ent of the nitro solvents.

For quite a while, I've been using several solvents and other items by Totally Dependable Products, Post Office Box 277, Zieglerville, Pennsylvania 19492. This includes their TDP SS1, a cleaner and solvent for blackpowder. It comes in a 5-ounce aerosol can with an applicator tube, and is unusual among the solvents in that it will not harm wood, rubber, painted surfaces, and most plastics. It also will not stain most fabrics, and yet it does a fine job of cleaning blackpowder residue. This performance is typical of all the TDP items. Apparently, anyone with the nerve to name their company "Totally Dependable Products" would have to be extra-sure that their stuff works!

At one time (perhaps still), the J. M. Bucheimer Company, Frederick, Maryland 21701, well-known for their holsters, offered a Cleaner and Patch Lubricant that also had penetrant

Totally Dependable Products calls its blackpowder solvent SS1. I have always found that TDP items live up to the company name.

The Bucheimer company is more noted for its leather goods and holsters, but they also have made a good blackpowder cleaner and patch lubricant.

qualities. After firing, a liberal spraying of the internal and external surfaces would allow a delay of several days before cleaning, with no rust. I've tried it, and it worked perfectly, but it's still best to clean muzzle-loaders at the end of the shooting day.

Jet-Aer has a G96-brand Black Powder Solvent and Patch Lubricant in an aerosol can, and this one also has metal fouling and penetrant action. All of the G96 products that I've used

work as their labels say. As we end our look at the blackpowder solvents, this seems a good place to comment on "penetrants." One of the best-known of these is WD-40 (Post Office Box 80607, San Diego, California 92138). When used as intended, to loosen screws or other parts seized by rust, it will do the job well. It is not, however, an efficient preservative.

A friend inherited a Remington Model 870 shotgun, and as he was primarily a handgunner,

Another combination solvent and patch lubricant that works well is this one by G96 (Jet-Aer).

Penetrants are fine when used for their specific purpose, but do not offer long-term protection. Two good ones are SS P by TDP, and WD-40.

he decided to put it away in a dry closet in his home. At this point, he made two mistakes. Thinking he was protecting it from rust, he sprayed it liberally with WD-40. Then, he zipped it into a vinyl case, and left it in the closet for several months. When it emerged from storage, the barrel and receiver had extensive areas of surface rust. We had to refinish it. What went wrong?

When used as the penetrant/lubricant it is, to free and temporarily lubricate rusted parts, WD-40 and similar solutions do a fine job. Their penetrating quality, though, requires a "thinness" that tends to work against functioning as a protective coating. Also, in the case of my friend's gun, there was a closed vinyl-covered case that trapped any ambient moisture inside, next to the steel of the barrel and receiver. Probably, on the day the gun was put away, there was high humidity. Even so, had the gun been

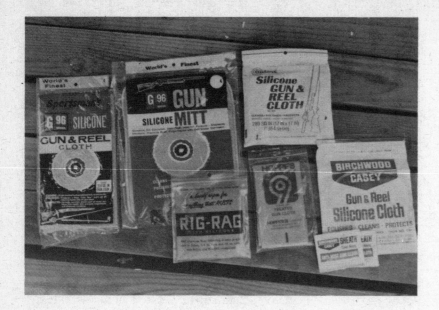

Most of the companies that make cleaning products offer handy cloths that are impregnated with protective elements. Here are a few, by G96, RIG, Outers, Hoppe's, and Birchwood Casey.

coated with RIG or some other good preservative, it would not have rusted.

Whenever I need a super-penetrant, I usually reach for an aerosol can of SS P, a special penetrant made by Totally Dependable Products. In workbench use, it has freed many rust-frozen screws. A completely rusted Spanish 25 automatic pistol was cycled and fired, without jamming, after just two squirts of SSP, one on each side at the lower edge of the slide. In other than firearms uses, I have restored non-running electric fans to perfect operation with a single application of SSP on the rotor shaft. Amazing stuff. One warning, though, about all of the penetrants: Don't use them, ever, in or around the magazine of an auto or the cylinder of a revolver. Their penetrant action can take them into the cartridges, and this can kill the primers. In later self-defense usage of the handgun, this could prove to be embarrassing. At least.

One of the most convenient innovations in cleaning and protection of the external surfaces of handguns is the chemically-treated cloth. In addition to lubricants, a principal ingredient of many gun-cloths is silicone. The Outers entry in this group is a 17-inch square of pure Canton flannel impregnated with silicone. It can even be washed without losing its polishing qualities.

Birchwood Casey's cloth is 14.4 by 15 inches, and it is also silicone-impregnated. Also from Birchwood Casey is a small "Sheath Take-Along Anti-Rust Cloth." It comes in a tear-pack, and has an oil-based impregnation. It's convenient for a pocket in the field, and is intended to be disposable.

The ingredients of Hoppe's treated cloth are not known, but from its texture I believe it also has silicone. Hoppe's also offers a small equivalent of the disposable cloth, theirs containing MDL (Moisture Displacing Lubricant). RIG Products has an oval pad of genuine sheepskin that is impregnated with silicone and lubricant, and this high-quality combination has the unlikely name of "RIG-Rag." I've kept one of these on top of my handgun cabinet for quite a while. The small disposable cloths are meant for field or range use, but the larger cloths are mainly used at home, to wipe down handguns after they have been handled.

There are two other cloths that should be mentioned, and each is a special-purpose type. The Wipe Away, by Belltown, Ltd., Route 37, Box 74, Sherman, Connecticut 06784, is specifically designed for lead removal. On the face of the cylinder, this cloth will just wipe the lead away, as its name implies. It can also be

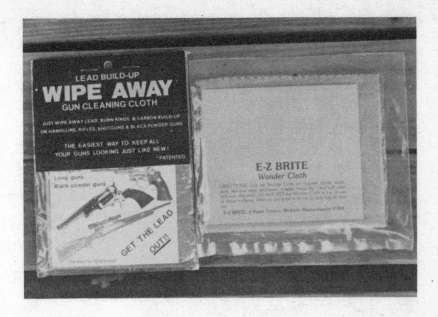

Two cloths with a similar purpose, the removal of lead and carbon from handgun surfaces. The E-Z Brite, though, should *not* be used on blued steel.

cut into small patches for removal of lead from the barrel and forcing cone. I don't know what's in it, but it works perfectly. Along with the lead smears, it even removes the "burn rings" from the front of the cylinder. At the time this is written, the Wipe Away cloth sells for $4.95, and its action is amazing.

The other cloth in this category is the E-Z Brite "Wonder Cloth," made by the E-Z Brite Company, 6 Susan Terrace, Woburn, Massachusetts 01801. It is also designed for the removal of lead and carbon deposits on revolvers, but *only* on stainless steel or nickel-plated guns. If you forget and use it on a blued surface, it will remove the blue! In addition to its lead-removal application, it will also do an excellent job on discolored brass fittings on muzzleloaders. I tried it on a brass-frame Spiller & Burr replica revolver, and it made it look like new. The E-Z Brite cloth sells for around $3, and it works fine, but remember—don't use it on a blued finish!

After a handgun is thoroughly cleaned, inside and out, there are only two main concerns: Protecting the external finish, and lubricating the internal parts for smooth operation. For the outside surfaces, there are quite a few good solutions available. While they differ in chemical

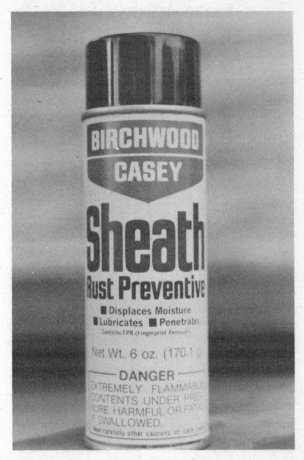

Among the protectants, Birchwood Casey Sheath is well-known as an effective solution.

MP-5 Oil by Beeman is a particularly fine lubricant and protectant.

Protectant/lubricant solutions by Totally Dependable Products include SS2 and SS2 Plus. Both are excellent.

make-up, most of them have similar functions. They have moisture-displacement properties, and some form of surface protectant. Some double as lubricants, and some have wax or grease ingredients.

Birchwood Casey Sheath is a dual protective coating and lubricant that is polarized to cling to all metal surfaces, and it also has a special ingredient that neutralizes and removes fingerprints. It is available in regular liquid and in

aerosol cans, and is harmless to the wood finish on grips, plastics, rubber, and fabrics. A non-aerosol liquid with practically identical qualities is offered by Beeman Precision Firearms, 47 Paul Drive, San Rafael, California 94903. It's called MP-5 Oil, the MP standing for "Metalophilic," a reference to its polarized molecules that seek metal surfaces and displace moisture.

Totally Dependable Products has two aerosol items in this category, their SS 2 All-Purpose

Hoppe's entries in the lubricating and protecting group are MDL, a rust inhibitor, and Dri-Lube with Teflon.

Outers has an aerosol Gun Oil, and their Teflon-content protectant is called TR-3.

Gun Lubricant, and SS 2 Lubricant Plus. Both come with an applicator tube. They are excellent protectants and lubricants, and they also have penetrant qualities. The Lubricant Plus seems to have somewhat more penetrant action, and also contains a moisture displacer. Both products are harmless to wood, rubber, painted surfaces, and most plastics, so the user need not be apprehensive if some of the solution gets on the grips. It should be pointed out, though, that

many of the protective solutions (and most of the solvents) can "spot" some types of plastic used for grips.

Hoppe's offers two dual-purpose protectant-lubricants in aerosol cans. One is called MDL (Moisture Displacing Lubricant), and the other is Dri-Lube, containing Du Pont Teflon. They are liquids when sprayed, but the liquids evaporate in seconds, leaving a dry surface (they contain no oils or silicones) that reduces friction and

RIG 2 is a protectant that I use with some frequency. The "dry" lube from RIG is called Moly Dri.

also guards the metal. Because the Teflon is in suspension, the can must be shaken between applications to insure that there is even distribution of the main element.

From Outers, we have an aerosol can with a tube applicator that is simply labeled "Gun Oil." It's also available as a non-aerosol liquid. This is another dual-purpose item, intended for use on both external surfaces and internal mechanisms. Since it is actually an oil, its lu-

bricating properties are superior to its protective qualities. For the latter, a better coating can be done with Outers Tri-Lube (TR-3). It contains Teflon, is a penetrant and lubricant, and provides a long-lasting protective film to the surface areas. Like some of the solvents, it contains 1,1,1-trichloroethane, so some caution should be observed in regard to the finish of wood grips, and some plastic grips.

There are several good products available from the RIG division of Mitann, Incorporated. Their dual-purpose lubricant/protectant is called RIG 2, a combination of oils, corrosion inhibitors, acid neutralizers, and waxes. It is also a moisture displacer. For quite a while, I've kept a soft flannel cloth sprayed with RIG 2 on the bookcase behind my desk, to wipe down any guns that I handle there. RIG also has a "dry" lubricant called Moly Dri, containing MoS_2 that forms a quick-drying non-oil lubricant film. It's especially suited for automatic pistols, particularly gas-operated guns such as the Heckler & Koch P7 and the Steyr GB, in areas where oil is not a desirable lubricant.

In the gas-operated pistols, oil in certain places can actually be detrimental to smooth operation. The gas chamber of the Steyr GB and the gas piston area of the HK P7 must be kept clean and dry. If these areas are oiled, the hot powder gases can bake oil-type lubricants into a hard scale that is difficult to remove. If this scale is allowed to build up, it can actually retard the movement of the slide. When no oil is applied in these locations, removal of the powder residue with a bronze or stainless-steel brush is relatively easy.

There is one product that could have been included in all of the previously-mentioned categories, because it does just about everything. It's Break-Free CLP, made by the San-Bar Corporation, 9999 Muirlands Boulevard, Irvine, California 92714. The CLP stands for "Cleaner-Lubricant-Preservative," and it can be employed for all three uses. It has ingredients with a neutral PH factor (neither acid nor caustic) that will easily remove all harmful firing

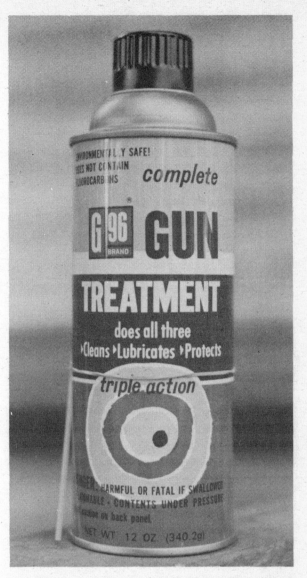

Break Free CLP has passed some impressive tests, including acceptance by the military. It's the nearest to an "all-around" solution.

An all-purpose lubricant and protectant is offered by G96 as their Complete Gun Treatment.

residue. Its lubricating qualities are excellent, and it retains all of its action at temperatures that would boil away or freeze other liquids. In laboratory tests of its preservative qualities, it prevented rust and corrosion for more than 900 hours in a humidity chamber, and for more than 100 hours in a 5 percent salt spray. It also has penetrant qualities, but not to the extent that it is likely to migrate and cause primer problems. Of course, it's always a good idea to keep *any* lubricant or preservative from extensive contact with cartridges. Break-Free lubricates immediately on application, but its action will actually improve after it has "cured" for a while. It has been widely accepted by civilian shooters, police, and the military.

An earlier generation of shooters prized sperm whale oil as the perfect lubricant. It had high adhesion to metal surfaces, resistance to extremes of temperature and pressure, and was

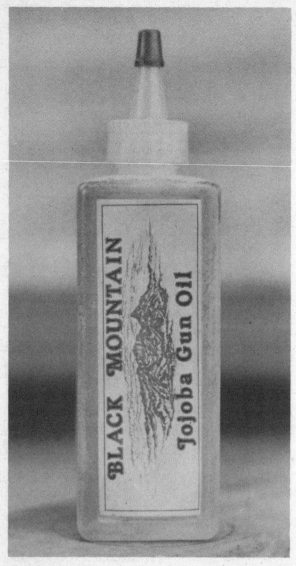

Amazing Jojoba Oil is a perfect chemical substitute for virtually unobtainable sperm oil.

an excellent non-corrosive agent. Unfortunately, it was obtainable from only one source—the sperm whale, a species now protected by many countries. By law, genuine sperm oil can be sold only in the state where the stock is located. When a small quantity can be found, the price will be substantial. Sperm oil also has some disadvantages. It doesn't keep well, and it has an unpleasant odor.

From an unlikely source, there is a liquid that is nearly the chemical twin of sperm oil. In the southwestern United States there is a plant called the jojoba (pronounced ho-HO-bah) that has long been known as a browse plant and ornamental shrub. Its scientific name is *Simmondsia chinensis*. In recent years, it has been cultivated for its beans, which produce a waxy oil. Jojoba oil has all of the excellent properties of sperm oil, without any of its disadvantages. It is odorless, and never turns rancid, even after long-term storage. Jojoba oil is a fine patch lubricant for blackpowder shooting, but this is only one of its many applications. As an internal lubricant, it adheres well to parts and is longlasting. When used as a protective coating, its waxy properties allow it to leave a non-sticky surface that will resist fingerprints. As a protectant, it works well not only on metal, but also on the wood of grips and on leather holsters. Quite a list of accomplishments, for something that comes from a scrubby little desert bush! It's been quite a while since I've been in touch with the company that produced it, as I had a good supply on hand, so I'll give both addresses, the producer and the marketing company, just in case: Tri-M Ranches, Route One, Box 539, Ramona, California 92065 and Black Mountain, 3190 Central Avenue, Spring Valley, California 92077.

The earliest handguns made of stainless steel sometimes had problems with "galling," the transfer of metal from one surface to another in areas of sliding or pivoting contact of parts. In current production of stainless steel handguns, this has been practically eliminated by the use of different stainless alloys for meeting parts. Even so, stainless steel has surface properties that are not the same as those of regular steel, and special lubricants have been developed for it. One of these that I've been using for a long time is CS Lubricant, made by CS Laboratories, 4219 South Walhaven Court, Las Vegas, Nevada 89103. It's sort of like a grease, but that doesn't exactly describe it. It's light blue in color, and has a consistency much like Noxzema facial cream. It adheres well to parts, and

For years, I've been using CS Lubricant in stainless steel handguns. A recent addition is +P Stainless Steel Lube by RIG.

does not migrate to other areas of the gun. Although it's designed for stainless steel, I often use it in regular steel handguns, especially as a lubricant for sear and hammer engagement.

Another lubricant for stainless steel was recently introduced by RIG Products. It's RIG +P Stainless Steel Lube, a dark brown grease-like material that's intended for the same applications as the product described above. I haven't yet used it as extensively as the other item, but in some test applications it worked well in both stainless steel and non-stainless handguns. Based on the performance of other RIG products, it should hold up in long-term use. Mentioning long-term use is a perfect introduction to the best storage preservative yet devised by man: RIG Universal Grease. This title is semi-redundant, as the letters in RIG originally stood for "Rust Inhibiting Grease."

Some years ago, in a magazine column, a reader who had difficulty with rust on guns in long storage wrote to ask "What do *you* use?" Answering truthfully, I replied in the column that I always used RIG. Unfortunately, at that time, RIG was not a regular advertiser in that particular magazine. Several other makers of preservatives were, and they were less than pleased with my answer. To preclude another

When a handgun is to be put away for storage, an application of RIG Universal will absolutely prevent any occurrence of rust.

flurry of stiffly-worded letters, let me say that there are several excellent preservatives, some of them already detailed on the preceding pages.

For lengthy storage, though, I still use RIG. It does have one disadvantage—it is a grease, and when it's applied to the external surfaces of a

For collector pieces that may be handled with some frequency, a good protectant is Formula 15 Gunwax. It can be used on both metal and the wood of grips, and is a fine fingerprint preventive.

handgun, the gun will be greasy to the touch. So, on guns that I will be using with some frequency, I use the other products. On guns that I'm putting away for quite a while, such as certain rare pieces in my "reference file," I've found that a coating of RIG is absolutely the best protection that can be obtained.

Collectors like to show their prized pieces, and some don't object to the guns being carefully handled by those who are sincerely interested. There is always, though, the worry of salt-laden fingerprints that can cause a surface spot in a relatively short time. While RIG is a superb protectant, its greasy properties count against it for display and handling. I have re-cently tried a product that may be a good alternative for this application: Formula 15 Gunwax, made by Frontier Products Company, 164 East Longview Avenue, Columbus, Ohio 43202. It's a blend of Carnauba wax and silicones, and it is applied in the same manner as similar waxes used on automobiles, furniture, and shoes. It not only protects against fingerprints, but also offers some protection against scratches. It works on both metal surfaces and wood grips, and can be left in matte form or buffed to a deep lustre. It's a very rich wax, not thinly formulated, and it works just as the maker claims. It is also relatively inexpensive.

Cleaning Methods

As mentioned at the start of this part of the book, every shooter has his own method of cleaning a handgun. This can range from a simple pass-through of a brush or a solvent-soaked patch to a complete detailed takedown and a pan-washing of all parts. The latter method is normally used only by gunsmiths, in cases where the gun has been submerged in water, or is being prepared for refinishing. A complete-takedown cleaning is also advisable once or twice a year if the handgun is usually carried in an open holster, in very humid or very dusty environments.

I have a friend who maintains and repairs oil

pumps on working wells, and he carries a holstered handgun as a snake deterrent. After a few months of open-holster/open-Jeep carrying, his 22 automatic pistol once refused to function at all. When I dismantled it, the dust deposits were found in amazing locations. One paste-like dust-and-oil combination inside the grip panel had jammed the disconnector in a depressed position. When the pistol was cocked, it wouldn't fire. My friend is an experienced shooter and outdoorsman, but he is not a gunsmith, so he brought the gun to me. After it was detail-stripped and cleaned, it worked perfectly. Then, I suggested that he get a flap-style holster.

Many handguns that are taken to a gunsmith for repair need only a thorough cleaning. This is most often true of 22 rimfire handguns, especially automatic pistols. In the short barrels of these guns, a small portion of the powder is not consumed. Also, the bullets of many 22 cartridges have a wax-like coating. Unburned powder flakes, bullet lubricants, and the oil used in the action combine to make a residue that is seldom completely removed in a routine cleaning. In cases of extreme build-up, it can retard or completely stop the functioning.

Revolvers are not immune to this condition, and in some cases it can apply even to center-fires. Some reloads, with certain types of powder, leave a sizable quantity of unburned powder flakes in the fired cases. When the cases are ejected from the cylinder, the mouths of the cartridge cases leave the chambers and drop some of the powder flakes on the ejector shaft. Its return transfers them to the underside of the ejector star. When there is enough build-up, the star will not seat properly in its recess, and the cylinder will bind.

Blackpowder handguns have their own set of rules. As any shooter of muzzle-loaders knows, these guns must be cleaned immediately after every day of shooting, before the acid residue can do its destructive thing. In fact, because of the rapid build-up of fouling, shooters will usually do a quick cleaning, or at least "run a patch," between groups during extensive shooting. This sort of interim cleaning is especially necessary when shooting a blackpowder revolver, as accumulation of residue at the front of the cylinder can retard its rotation.

For all types of handguns, my own cleaning methods fall somewhere between the minimum described earlier and the gunsmith's complete takedown. Those who have developed their own methods and variations over the years are not doing it wrong. If your system of cleaning gets all of the gunk out, keep doing it that way. Those who are just beginning in the sport of shooting may find the methods shown and described in the following pages to be a helpful guide. I use them on my own handguns.

Autoloading Pistols

For cleaning, one of the good things about automatics is that most of them can be easily field-stripped without tools. Except for the Ruger double actions, this is generally not true of revolvers. Field-stripping normally entails removal of the slide or bolt, the recoil spring assembly, and usually the barrel. In pistols that have a non-removable barrel, removal of the slide will at least give direct access to the barrel, chamber, and feed ramp. While the factory owner's manuals supplied with most pistols rarely detail complete takedown, all of them give instructions for field-stripping. If you don't have the original manual, there are books (my Firearms Assembly/Disassembly series by DBI, for example) that have this information. Assuming that you have mastered simple takedown, here are my cleaning methods for auto pistols:

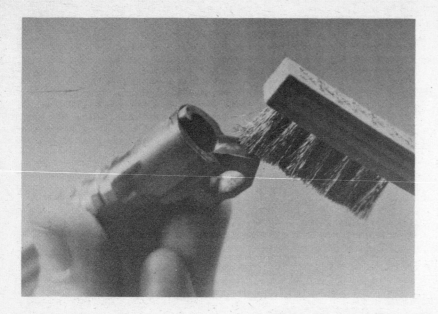

1. Brush the powder residue from the rear face of the barrel and the feed ramp. This can be done with a nylon or fiber brush or a toothbrush and some solvent, but I prefer to do it "dry", using the Brownells stainless steel brush, as shown.

2. (Below) With a dry bronze or stainless steel brush of the proper size, brush out the bore, from the chamber end if possible. Here, again, it can be done with a nonmetallic brush and solvent, if you prefer.

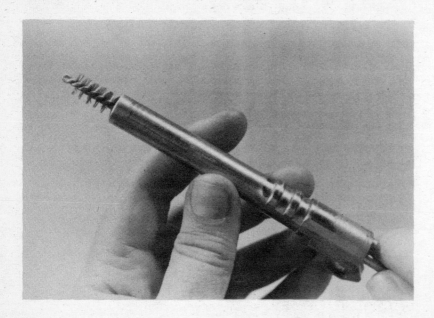

3. When brushing the bore with a bronze or stainless steel brush, be sure that the entire brush exits the bore before drawing it back through. Otherwise, the laid-back bristles will make reversal difficult. If the barrel is "soft", as in many 22 pistols, reversing the brush in the bore may even cause damage to the rifling. When cast-bullet reloads have been fired, you can see tiny flakes of lead expelled as the brush comes out the muzzle.

4. (Above) The chamber is very slightly larger than the bore, and a bore brush of the proper caliber will not do a good job of cleaning the chamber. When the caliber range allows, I use a brush of the next size upward to clean the chamber. A 44 caliber brush is shown in this 9mm chamber. Use a turning motion for easy insertion and removal.

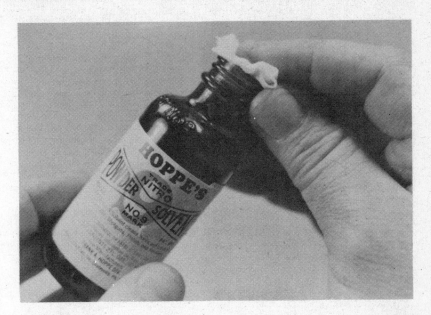

5. (Above, right) If a slotted patch tip is used, the patch can be put through the slot and dipped in the solvent bottle. It shouldn't be re-dipped after a run-through, though, or the solvent will be fouled by residue. When a jag tip is used, the patch can be conveniently soaked by folding it twice, holding it as shown, and tipping the bottle.

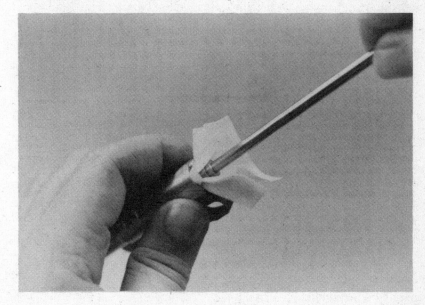

6. (Right) Centering the treated patch on the chamber, use the jag tip to push it to the muzzle, but stop before it exits the bore.

7. (Above) When the patch is visible at the muzzle, as shown, reverse the stroke and pull it back to the chamber end, but not out of the chamber. Repeat this run-through several times, keeping the patch in the bore.

8. (Below) When the patch is finally pushed out, discoloration of powder and metal residue removed by the solvent will be obvious. Note that there is always some patch darkening from the solvent, but the difference can be seen. Repeat the process with fresh solvent-soaked patches until one comes out clean.

9. (Above) Brush the top of the frame in the chamber area, and the feed ramp on the frame, if your pistol has this feature. On some guns, the entire feed ramp is on the underlug of the barrel.

10. (Below) With a bore brush of appropiate size, brush the front of the magazine well in the frame. A surprising amount of powder residue is found in this area.

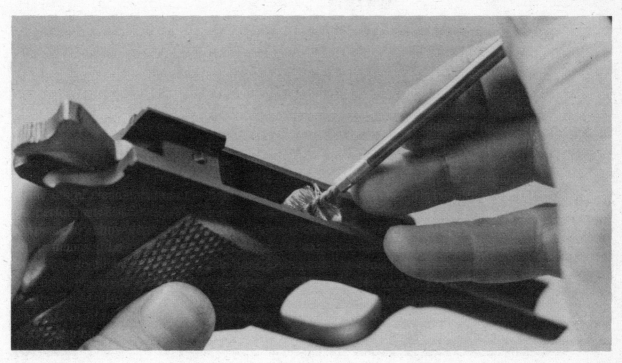

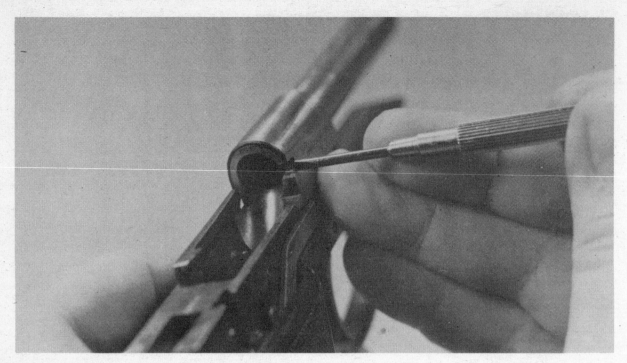

11. (Above) If the chamber of the barrel has an extractor recess, use a tool, such as the small screwdriver shown here, to clear it of any residue.

12. (Below) Brush the underside of the slide in the breech block area, being sure that the residue is also removed from the recesses on each side.

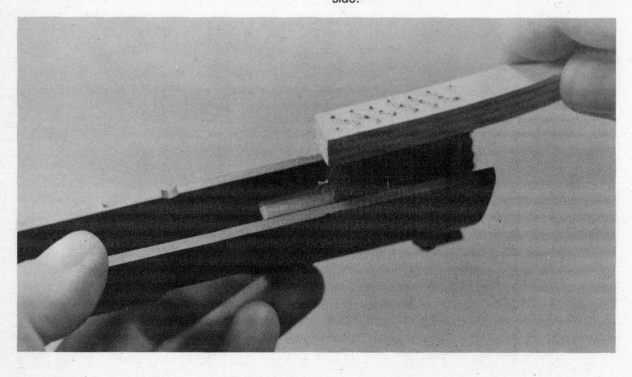

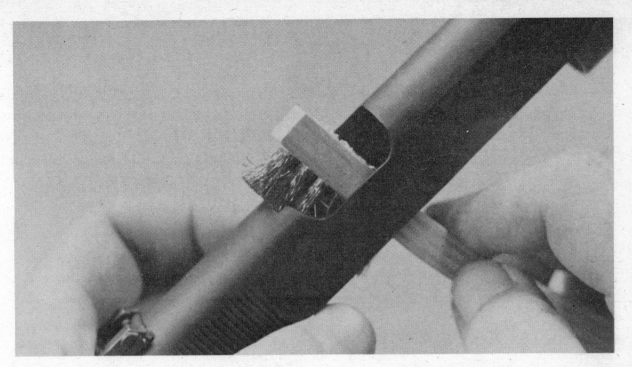

13. (Above) Brush the breech face area in the slide, and the inner walls on each side. If residue is allowed to build up here, it can affect feeding.

14. (Below) In 22 rimfire pistols, the rim step below the chamber can accumulate lead shavings. Use a small tool to remove it. A dental tool from the set offered by Brownells is shown here, but a very small screwdriver will also do the job.

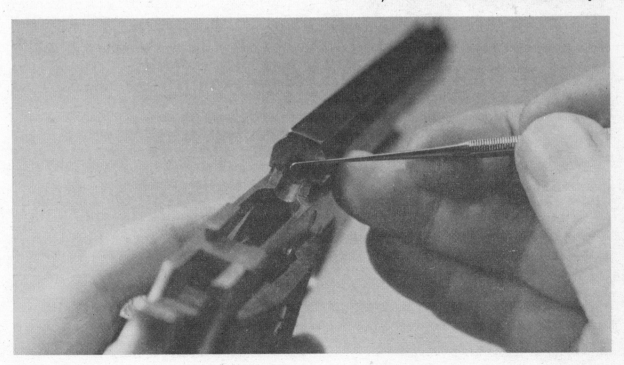

15. Occasional cleaning of any dismountable magazine is a good idea, but in 22 rimfire pistols it becomes an imperative. With the magazine dissassembled, the spring can usually be cleaned by passing it through a cloth. The magazine follower should be brushed, as shown.

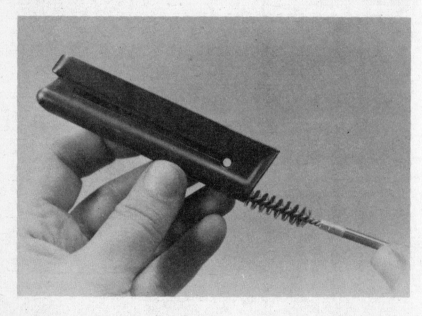

16. The body of the magazine is cleaned by using a bore brush of appropriate size. A brush of smaller dimensions must be used for the rear portion when the magazine is the type shown.

17. Some residue will have drifted down to the floorplate of the magazine, and it should be brushed before reassembly.

18. (Above) It's not necessary after every shooting session, but occasionally the grips should be removed, and the area they cover brushed. This is especially important if the gun is carried for long periods next to clothing, or in a dusty environment. Fabric lint or dust can build up inside the grips, and if this becomes severe, it can affect the mechanism.

19. (Right) One of the often-ignored important cleaning points is the inside of the extractor beak. A residue build-up here can interfere with proper contact of the extractor beak with the rim of the cartridge, causing an extraction failure. Use a small sharp tool, such as the dental tool shown, to remove any residue. In cases of heavy deposits in this area, the extractor should be removed and its channel in the slide cleaned.

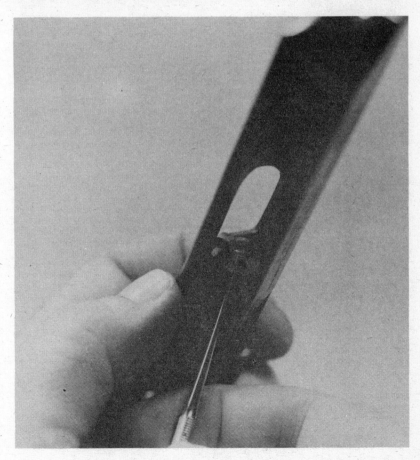

20. (Left) The gas-locked pistols have special cleaning requirements, in addition to the regular procedures. The ported gas deposits a film of residue on the components of the gas system, and normal cleaning procedures do not remove it easily. Here, a stainless steel brush is used to clean the gas piston of a Heckler & Koch P7 pistol.

21. (Below) The gas chamber of the Heckler & Koch P7 can be cleaned by using a bronze or stainless steel bore brush of the proper size. The gas port in the barrel, just forward of the chamber, can be cleaned with a pipe cleaner bent into an L-shape.

22. The Steyr GB pistol vents gas onto the forward outside portion of the barrel. There is ample space in this area, so the build-up is not harmful. A stainless steel brush removes the residue easily.

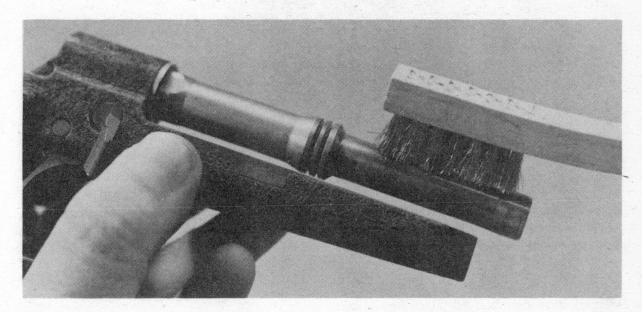

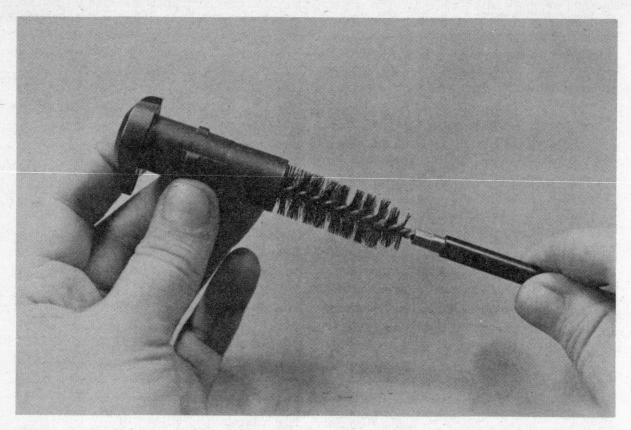

23. Cleaning the gas chamber of the Steyr GB is done best with the special stainless steel brush that is supplied with the gun, as shown. If the factory brush is unavailable, a bronze or stainless steel shotgun bore brush will work. One thing to remember about the gas-locked pistols:

After cleaning, the components of the gas system should be left absolutely *dry*. Any lubricant left on these parts will be baked by the heat of the powder gases into a hard scale that is very difficult to remove.

24. When a pressurized solvent is used in conjunction with a slotted patch tip, the solvent can be easily applied as shown, after the patch is in the slot. Use just enough to saturate the patch, and use the same run-through method as described with the jag-type tip.

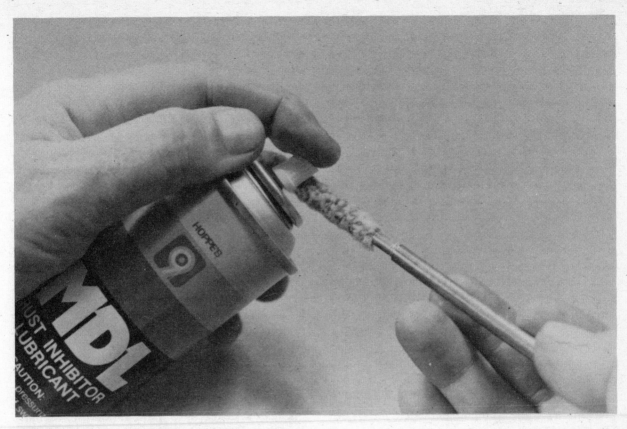

25. (Above) After cleaning, a preservative is applied to the bore by using a mop attachment. Its tufted surface gives a more even distribution than a patch.

26. (Below) Preservative-treating the bore with a mop attachment requires only a single pass-through and return. Before shooting again, it's best to run a dry patch through the bore to remove the protective coating.

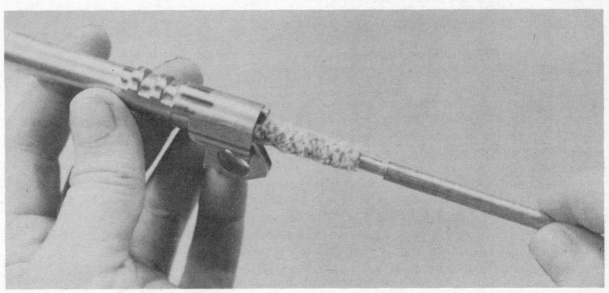

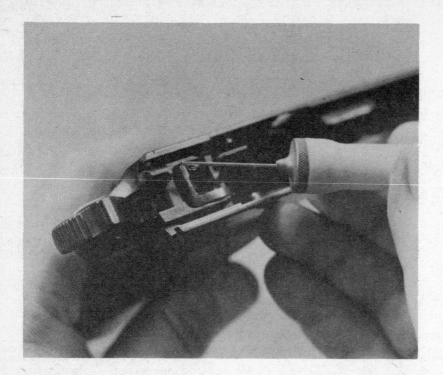

27. Internal oiling should be done very sparingly. Just a drop on the point of sear and hammer engagement, the slide rails, and the disconnector will be enough. A pin-point oiler of the type shown makes it easier to limit the amount. When the pistol has a double action trigger system, its components should also be lightly oiled, especially in the area of the trigger bar or bars.

28. (Below) Applying a preservative to the external surfaces can be done by direct spraying, as shown, but with some solutions, contact with plastic grips should be avoided. My own method is usually to spray a small amount on a metal surface, then spread it with a fingertip. An alternative is to spray the preservative on a soft cloth, then use it to apply a coating to the gun.

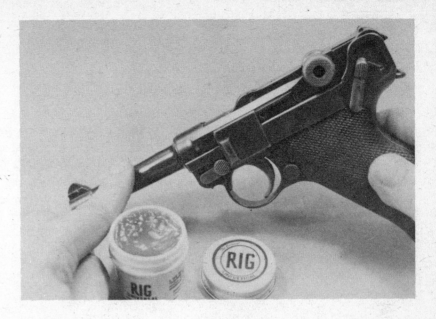

29. For long-term storage of any handgun, especially collector pieces, there is nothing better than RIG Universal. The best way I have found to apply this Rust Inhibiting Grease is with a fingertip.

30. Many shooters feel that stainless steel pistols, such as the American Arms Eagle shown, call for a special lubricant. CS Lubricant was developed especially for stainless steel, and I use it often. A small amount, as shown, is applied in the usual places. The slide rails are particularly important. CS Lubricant is also excellent for use in non-stainless pistols.

Revolvers

As mentioned a few pages back, the Ruger double action revolvers can be field-stripped with relative ease, and in modern cylinder-type handguns they are unique in this respect. For normal cleaning of revolvers, takedown is not really necessary. If it's wanted, the crane and cylinder assembly of most revolvers can be removed by taking out a single screw. Actually, the most that will need to be done is an occasional removal of the grips. All other cleaning operations can be accomplished by just swinging out the cylinder. Here are my cleaning methods for revolvers:

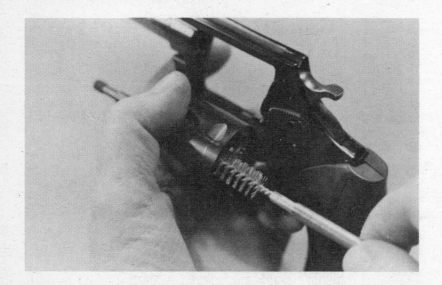

1. For dry-brushing revolver cylinder chambers, use a bronze or stainless steel brush that is slightly larger than the bore. Here, a 45 brush is used in a 44 chamber.

2. Use a stainless steel brush (or the Wipe Away cloth) to remove the lead and powder residue from the front face of the cylinder.

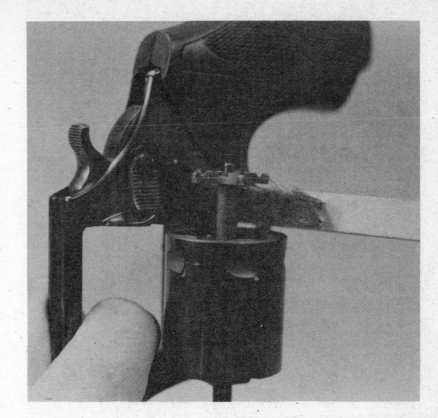

3. Brush the ejector shaft, the underside of the ejector star, and its recess in the cylinder. Unburned powder flakes or other residue that are allowed to build up in this area can cause the cylinder to bind.

4. In any revolver that has recesses in the cylinder for the cartridge heads, use a tool to remove any residue from each recess. This is particularly important in 22 rimfire guns, in which rapid build-up is possible.

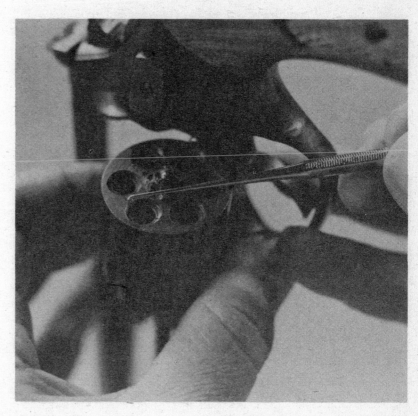

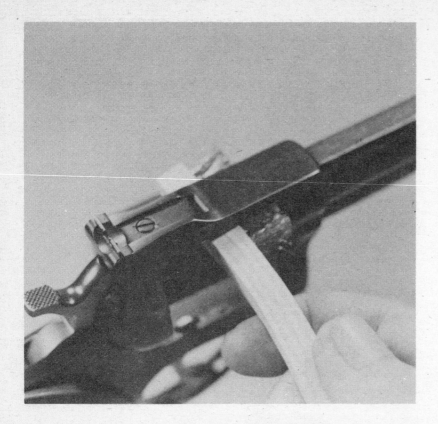

5. Brush the rear face of the barrel, the front strap of the frame, and the inside of the top strap. If there is noticeable lead deposit in the forcing cone of the barrel, use the Lewis Lead Remover, as described earlier.

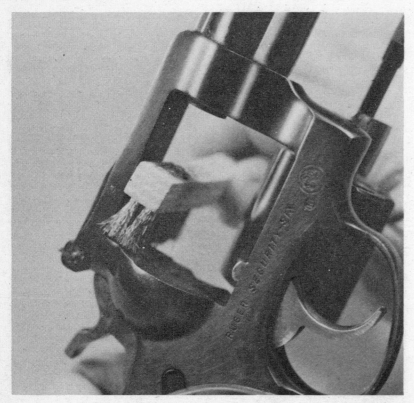

6. Brush the breech face and the rear inner portion of the top strap. Most of the residue will be concentrated in the area of the firing pin aperture. Special attention should be given to the top of the cylinder hand slot.

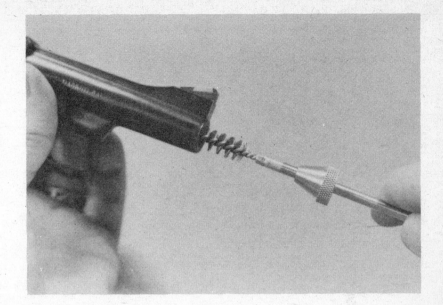

7. Using a dry bronze or stainless steel brush of the proper size, brush out the bore. Note the muzzle guard, which moves freely on the cleaning rod.

8. When the brush has entered the bore, muzzle guard should be snugged into the muzzle. As the brush emerges in the cylinder space, take care that its steel tip does not strike the breech face, to avoid damage to the firing pin aperture. The leather breech face shield shown will prevent any danger of this. Made by Don Moore (he calls it the Protector), it costs about $2. The address is: Moore Leather, 5183 Woodland Way, Eureka, CA. 95501.

9. When a jag-type cleaning rod tip is used, an easy way to saturate the patch is to fold it twice, hold it on the solvent bottle, and tip the bottle.

10. Using a slotted tip, the solvent can be sprayed on the patch after it's in the slot. Or, the patch and tip can be dipped directly into a solvent bottle. If this is done, though, a used patch should not be re-dipped, as this will contaminate the remaining solvent.

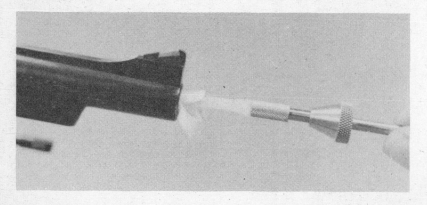

11. As the patch is started in the bore, some solvent will be squeezed out of it, so take care that the excess doesn't drop on anything it might mar or stain.

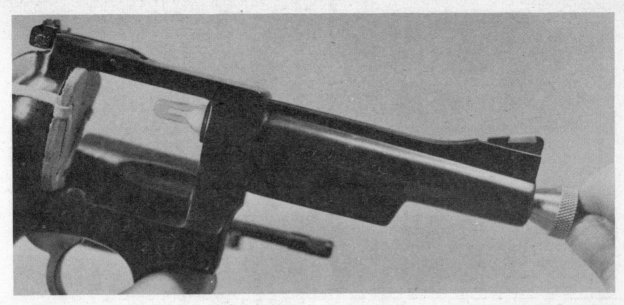

12. (Above) After the patch has entered the bore, snug the guard into the muzzle and hold it there as the patch is worked back and forth. Better contact and scrubbing action will be obtained if the direction is reversed when the patch is just visible in the cylinder space, as shown. If it's very tight, though, it may be necessary to push it completely out of the bore before reversal.

13. The Ox-Yoke Two-Way Tip, with its jag flanges fore and aft, is designed for a complete push-through before reversal. In both directions, there is good patch contact with the bore, especially when you use the unique slit patches made for it.

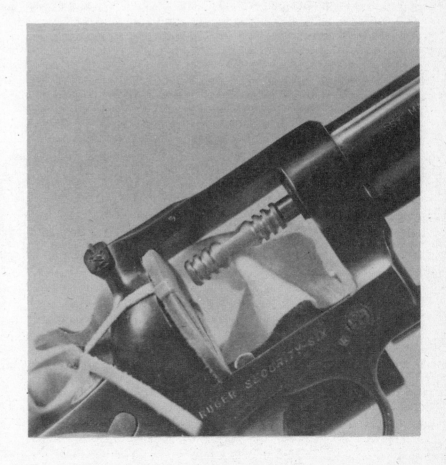

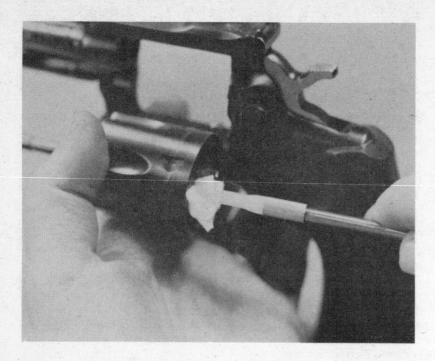

14. With a solvent-saturated patch in the cylinder chambers, use both a push-through and a turning motion, to insure patch contact with the steps in the chambers.

15. (Below) If the revolver is carried next to clothing or in a dusty environment, fabric lint or dust can combine with lubricant inside the grip panels. An extensive build-up can affect the mechanism. The grips should be removed occasionally, and frame brushed or otherwise cleaned.

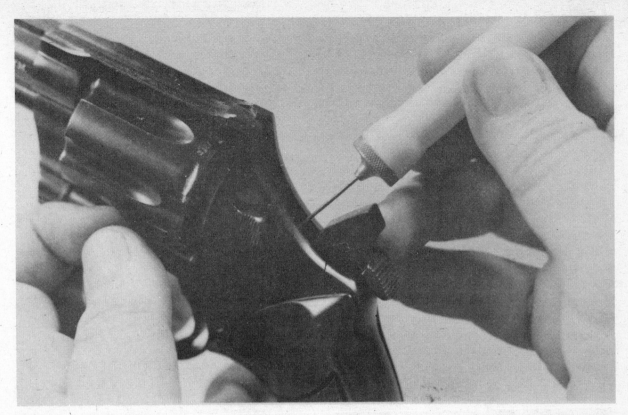

16. (Above) After cleaning, apply a drop or two of lubricant to the front of the double action lever on the hammer, as shown. Normal working of the action will transfer the lubricant to the sear surfaces of the hammer and trigger. Avoid over-oiling. A pin-point oiler, like the one shown, makes it easier to control the amount applied.

17. Apply a drop or two of lubricant to the front of the cylinder arbor. Cylinder rotation will bring the lubricant into the interior of the arbor tunnel in the cylinder.

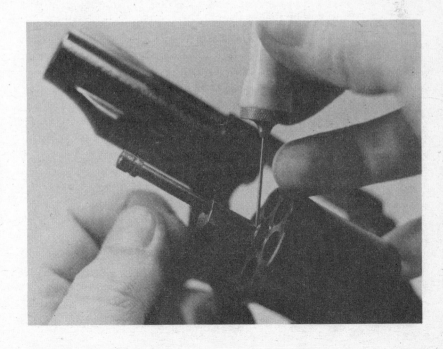

18. Lightly oil the front of the cylinder hand. In some revolvers, it will be necessary to cock the hammer to expose this area. If the hammer has an interlock with the cylinder latch, depress the latch to allow cocking the hammer with the cylinder swung out.

19. (Above) A mop attachment is the best way to apply a preservative to the bore. The mop has a tufted surface that gives better distribution than a patch. A single pass-through and return is all that's necessary—if the mop is properly saturated. Before the gun is fired again, a dry patch should be run through the bore to remove the protectant. It will do no harm if it's light, but it can affect the accuracy of the first shot.

20. If the external protectant used is harmless to the wood or plastic of the grip panels, it can be sprayed on directly, as shown. I usually spray a small amount on the metal, then spread it with a fingertip. It can also be applied to a soft cloth, then the cloth is used to wipe down the gun.

21. (Above) Collectors who handle their prized pieces often might want a non-grease alternative to RIG. For them, there is Formula 15 Gunwax, easily applied with a fingertip or cloth. It can be used on both wood and metal, and gives excellent fingerprint protection.

22. (Below) In addition to the CS Lubricant described earlier, there are other specialized products that are excellent for the stainless steel revolver. Two shown are Break Free CLP, and RIG + P Stainless Steel Lube.

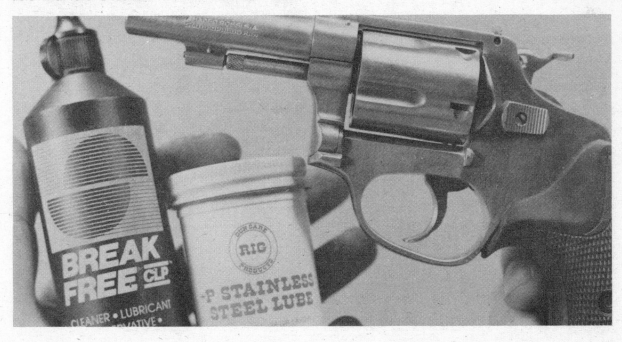

Blackpowder Handguns

There are muzzle-loading handguns with multiple barrels, pepperboxes, and other odd variations, but for our purpose here, three basic types will be shown: The single-shot pistol in flintlock and percussion, and the percussion revolver. Those who shoot muzzle-loaders usually need no instructions on takedown. These guns are usually designed for easy dismantling, and an occasional total-disassembly cleaning is recommended for all blackpowder guns. There is, of course, nothing wrong with cleaning by the old method, with hot water and soap. It worked fine for the pioneers, and it will still do the job. I have always preferred to use the modern equipment and chemicals that are available. Here are my blackpowder cleaning methods:

1. At some point in the cleaning of a single-shot percussion pistol, it will be necessary to remove the nipple, for cleaning of the drum area and the nipple itself. When using a pressurized can of solvent, I clean the nipple by squirting the solvent through it. A pipe cleaner is then used to remove any residue that is left.

2. (Above) Michaels of Oregon (Uncle Mike's) offers a good barrel flusher unit that consists of neoprene rubber tubing and a threaded fitting that is matched to the nipple threads in the drum. A rubber O-ring seals it when its knurled collar is turned to tighten it in place. Cleaning solution is then put in a container, such as a coffee-can, and the free end of the tube is submerged in it. As a tight patch is run back and forth in the bore, siphoning action pulls the solution in to fill the barrel, then expels it into the container. It works beautifully, and it keeps the mess away from the lock and the wood.

3. (Right) Ordinary bore brushes can be used in muzzle-loaders, but it's best to use specialized blackpowder brushes that are exactly fitted to the bore, allowing easy reversal for extraction.

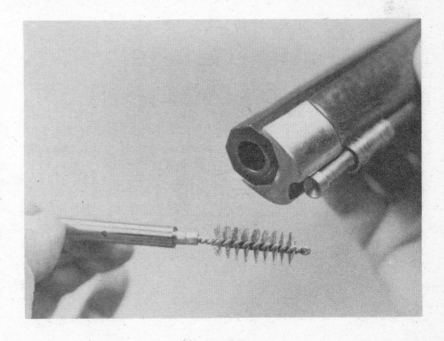

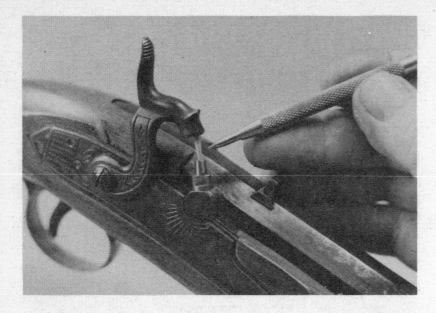

4. If the Michaels barrel-flusher unit is not used, my first cleaning step is to plug the nipple. One good way is to insert the broken-off tip of a round toothpick in the nipple, then let the hammmer down gently to hold it in place, as shown.

5. (Below, left) With the nipple plugged, apply three or four squirts of solvent directly to the bore. Insert just the tip of the applicator in the muzzle, to give good distribution in the bore. The amount of solvent applied will vary with the length of the barrel. Keep the muzzle elevated, to keep the solvent from running out.

6. Use a brush of the proper size to vigorously brush the bore. The brush will pick up solvent from the inside of the bore and the small quantity pooled in the chamber area. Note the non-conical muzzle guard shown, designed to be reversible for two calibers.

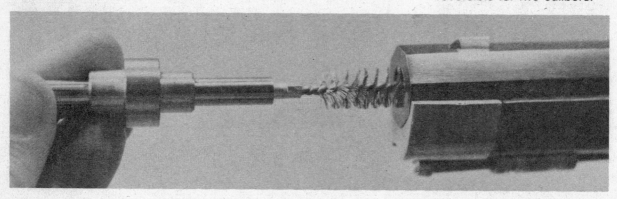

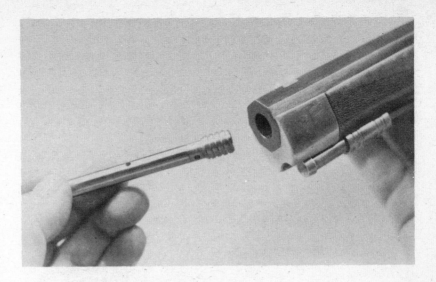

7. Just as with the brushes, blackpowder cleaning jags must be carefully fitted to particular bore sizes. If it's too large, the patch and jag can jam in the bore. If the jag is too small, the patch can detach from it, requiring extraction with a special tip.

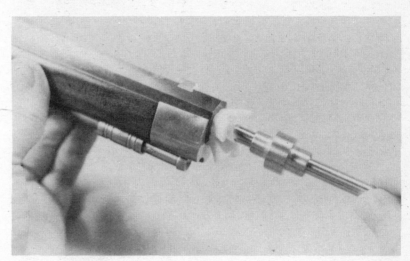

8. With the saturated patch centered over the bore, the jag tip pushes it in. The previous solvent soaking and brushing will have loosened the fouling, but it will still take several patches before the bore is clean. When the patch has entered, the muzzle guard should be snugged into the muzzle and held there.

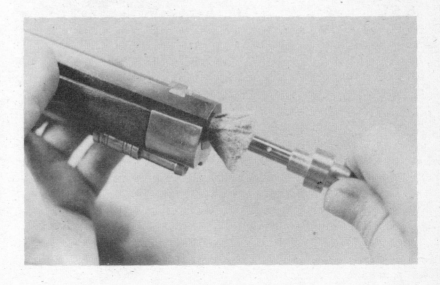

9. The patch is shown after a single pass through the bore. The process is repeated, with successive fresh patches, until one comes out clean. It may be necessary to add more solvent. A jag-type cleaning rod tip must be used, because a slotted tip will not bring the patch into contact with the rear wall of the chamber.

10. A stainless steel brush does an excellent job of cleaning the obvious residue from the pan of a flintlock, but the area should still be scrubbed with solvent, to combat the acid of blackpowder film.

11. (Below) When preparing to clean bore of a flintlock pistol, the touch-hole can be plugged in the same manner as described for the caplock, with a piece of round toothpick. In this case, a longer piece is used. Frizzen can be lowered on it to hold it in place.

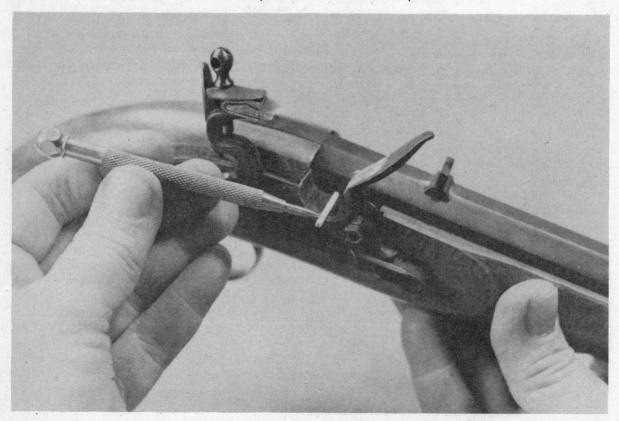

12. (Above) After the bore is cleaned, a solvent-saturated pipe cleaner is used to clear residue from the touch-hole. As noted above, the entire lock area should be scrubbed with solvent. With some frequency, the lock and the barrel should be removed from the wood, and all internal and external surfaces should be cleaned and treated with a preservative.

13. While it's not necessary for every cleaning, the nipples should occasionally be removed from the cylinder of a blackpowder revolver for individual cleaning, by the method already described.

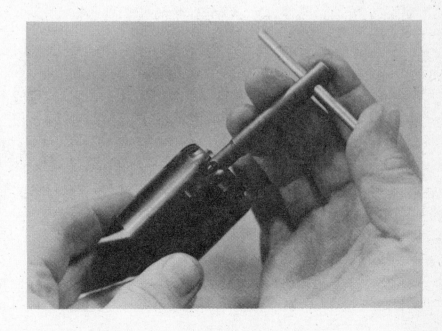

14. (Above) One chamber at a time, apply solvent directly to chambers of the cylinder. This should be done over a spread newspaper, or outdoors, as some solvent will leak out the nipple.

15. (Below) With a bronze or stainless steel brush of the proper size, brush out the chamber. Repeat the solvent and brush treatment in each chamber.

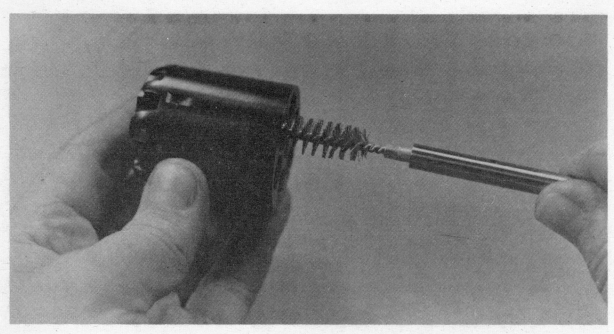

16. With a jag tip and solvent-soaked patches, clean each chamber thoroughly, until the patches show no black residue. Additional application of solvent may be necessary.

17. Brush out the bore, then run solvent-soaked patches through it until a fresh patch comes out clean. While this is done, the muzzle-guard should be held in place to protect the rifling from the moving rod.

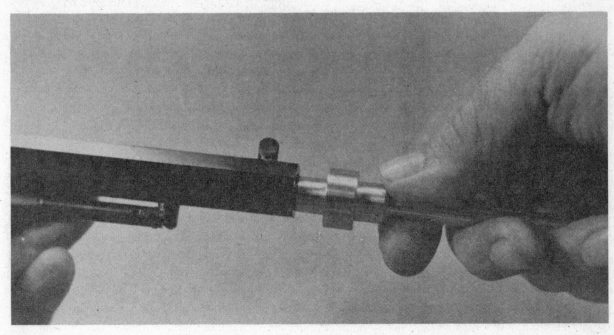

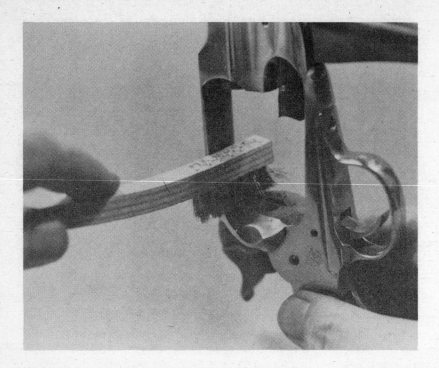

18. With a brush and solvent, clean the residue from the breech face and the surrounding area.

19. (Below) Brush the rear face of the barrel, the top strap of the frame (in non-Colt-pattern guns), and the rear tip of the loading plunger, using solvent.

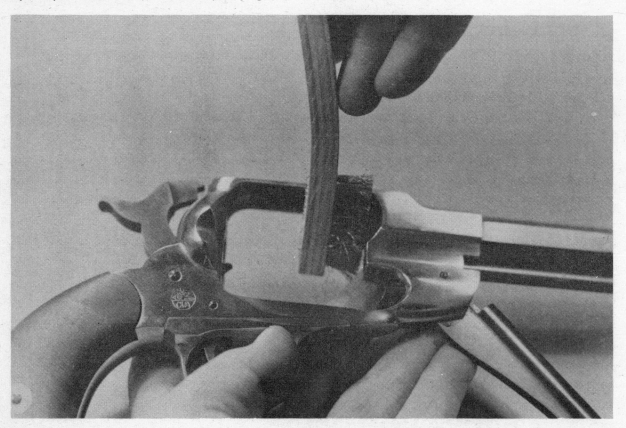

20. Clean the hammer nose and the front face of the hammer with a brush and solvent. A smaller brush, such as a child-size toothbrush, can be used to clean the hammer recess in the frame.

21. (Below) Use solvent and a brush to clean the rear face of the cylinder, with particular attention to the ratchet and the nipple recesses.

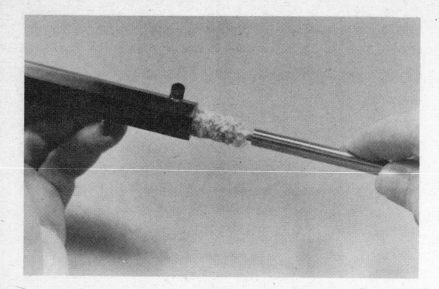

22. After cleaning, use a mop attachment to apply preservative to the bore and the cylinder chambers. Apply a drop or two of a good lubricant to the lower front of the hammer, the front of the cylinder hand, and the cylinder arbor.

23. (Below) If the gun is not to be used for a while, apply a surface protectant—even brass surfaces, such as the frame of this CVA Remington copy, need this protection. Fingerprints will often act on brass even more quickly than on steel. When the gun is to be fired again, it is particularly important in blackpowder arms to clean out the chamber or chambers with a dry patch, as lubricants can cause misfiring. After the protectant is swabbed out, snap a percussion cap on each nipple to clear away any oil that may remain.

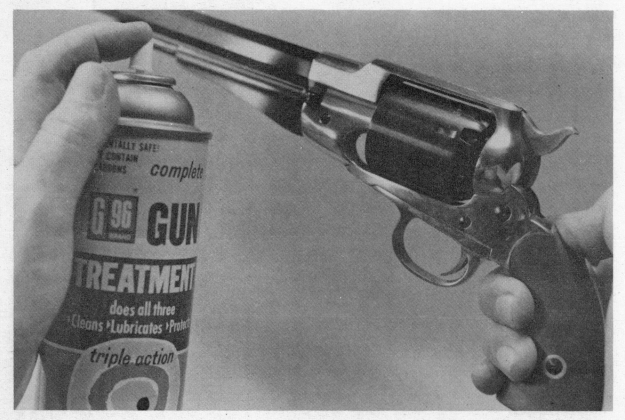

Section Three

Gun Refinishing

QUESTIONS ABOUT refinishing are most often concerned with three points: When it should be done, whether it will lower the value of the handgun, and finally, which finish to choose. We'll deal with the first two here, and the third one will be covered in the descriptions of the various finishes available. There is one other recurring question that should be answered: Is it possible to give a good finish to an entire handgun by using cold blue? My quick general answer to this one is "Not really."

"Cold blue," as its name implies, is a liquid or paste rapid-oxidizing agent that is very useful for touching up small areas of wear, or small parts, such as screw heads. If an entire handgun has been carefully polished to the bare steel, mirror-bright, and if a cold blue is applied rapidly and evenly, it's possible to impart a fairly good finish. The catch is, that it won't last. Cold blue lacks the depth of the hot-bath process used by manufacturers and gunsmiths, and the high spots and corner edges will begin to wear off almost immediately. Since a complete high-

polish is the most difficult part of any refinishing job, it's a shame to waste the effort by applying cold blue.

Getting back to the first question, when should a handgun be refinished? First, let's establish that we're now talking about practical and currently-made guns that exist in large quantity, not those that have collector value. We'll get to those a little further on. When a handgun is in constant use, whether in law enforcement or sporting endeavors, some wear to the external finish is inevitable. Even plating is not immune to wear. A blued finish will, of course, begin to show it sooner.

Areas of bare steel will eventually start to become evident on the sides of a revolver barrel at the muzzle, and at the front and rear edges of the cylinder. On an automatic pistol, the sides of the slide at the muzzle and all of the squared edges will be the first obvious locations. In both handgun types, any part of the grip frame that is not covered by the grip panels will wear from handling, and from contact with perspiration on

Section Three: Refinishing

An original factory finish, such as the nickel plating on this Colt Trooper Mark V, can never be exactly duplicated. However, an expert refinisher can come very close to matching it. Some manufacturers still offer factory refinishing.

the hand. In the other locations mentioned, holster wear is a factor. This occurs even when the holster is a high-quality rig, lined in orthopedic elk leather.

When this wear has progressed to the point that there is bare steel showing in several places, then the handgun is a candidate for refinishing. No matter how well-protected its surface by lubricants, bare steel has a tendency to be afflicted by surface rust. Even a light sprinkling of surface rust can cause minute pitting of the steel. So, to prevent this, a new finish is applied. Some choose a re-application of the original finish, while others may decide to change to an alternative finish that offers a greater degree of durability.

When the handgun is a currently-made piece by a well-known manufacturer, it is sometimes possible to obtain factory refinishing. The advantages of this are that the gun will be handled only by the people who made it, and the finish will, in effect, be the same as when the gun was new, if there are no deep pits on the surface. It should be noted, though, that not all manufacturers offer a factory refinishing service. Anyone who has this in mind should contact the maker of his handgun, and inquire about availability of this service and the price. Another

point to keep in mind is that factory refinishing usually takes somewhat longer than having it done locally.

Choosing a refinisher can be even more critical than choosing a gunsmith. When a mistake is made in a mechanical repair, it can usually be made right. With a refinishing mistake, though, the damage may not be reversible. The chemical and physical application of blue, the "hot bath," is a fairly straight-forward process. As long as the chemical quantities and the temperature of the solution are maintained at the proper levels, everything should come out all right. The point that separates the amateur from the professional is the preparation of the surface. Precision polishing of steel and other materials is an art, and not all practitioners are artists.

There are several areas in which an inept polishing job will be apparent. Screw heads are particularly revealing. Amateurs will often round the edges of the screw slots, instead of leaving them sharp. This also applies to other areas of the handgun. For example, the edge where the side flat of the slide on an auto or the frame on a revolver meets the curvature of the top. A non-professional will round this edge, every time. The flats themselves are also an important point—they should be absolutely flat,

This well-worn Savage pistol was photographed before refinishing. There were many scratches, areas of bare steel, and some surface rust. Originally, the gun had been blued.

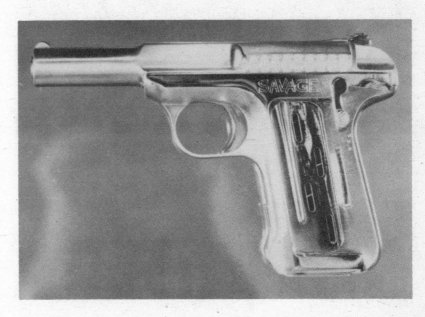

Refinished in a combination of satin and bright chrome by Dick Floyd, the old Savage has a totally changed appearance. New grip panels are yet to be added.

with no waves or dips, and this is difficult to accomplish. Finally, the markings on the gun should be preserved. I have seen amateur refinishing jobs on which the factory markings were either barely discernible, or entirely removed.

In my part of the country, gun people are fortunate in having the services of Richard A. Floyd, 5205 Sherbrook Road, Evansville, Indiana 47710. For gunsmiths and gun shops in an ever-widening area, he has become *the* refinish-

er, to the point that the rest of us have virtually stopped doing it. And, Dick is an artist. He can be trusted to deliver the finished job with all screw slots sharp, flat areas flat, and markings legible. His shop is equipped to provide either a high-polish or a matte surface, or a combination of the two. At the present time, he does only blue and nickel plating. I often plead with him to again offer his superb chrome, but so far I haven't convinced him. Decorative chrome, he

Here is a view of the same Savage pistol, this photo made some 10 years after the refinishing. The custom grips were made by the author from two sides of the same walnut block.

The contrast of polished and matte texture can also be done in blue, as illustrated by this Stenda pistol. Walnut custom grips by the author, blue by Dick Floyd.

says, requires a slightly more involved process, and right now his backlog of work just won't allow the extra time involved.

I used the term "decorative chrome" to separate this finish from the "hard chrome" finishes such as Armoloy. One of my reasons for wanting Dick to do chrome plating again is that the white color of chrome is a perfect match for polished aluminum alloy. Two pistols that were chromed for me by Dick deserve more of a de-

scription than the photo captions. One is a Beretta Model 948 in 22 Long Rifle chambering. After several years of carrying it as a camping piece, the blue on its barrel and slide was well-worn, and most of the black anodizing was gone from the grip frame. After a few days in the outback, the exposed steel areas would begin to show surface rust.

When this gun was refinished, the steel parts were done in chrome plating. The barrel, the

Another example of the matte and high polish combination, on a 25 CZ Model 1945 pistol. The blue is by Dick Floyd. Note that the factory markings, even though none too deep on this gun, were preserved.

Among currently-made new guns, the matte/polished pattern is often used, as on this Arminex Trifire. The author is a design consultant to Arminex, Ltd. Note the serial number of the gun shown.

side flats of the slide, and the magazine body were finished bright, and the other steel parts were given a matte chrome finish. The alloy frame was simply polished bright and left bare, and it's still perfect, 15 years later. The color of the polished alloy exactly matches the chromed parts.

The other gun that was done in a similar pattern of chrome was a Savage Model 1908 in 32 caliber. In this case, all parts were steel. The barrel, enclosed in this pistol except at the muzzle and ejection port, was polished and left bare, because the cycling of the slide would have soon left bearing marks on plating. Most of the external surfaces were done in matte chrome, with high polish on the side flats of the frame, the magazine body, the cocking lever, the trigger, safety lever, and the magazine catch. It's an attractive combination.

A similar contrasting pattern can be done in

Some of the new handguns on today's market, especially those designed for the police and military, have a matte finish on all surfaces. Shown is a SIG/Sauer P226 pistol.

blue. I have a 32 Stenda pistol that was done for me several years ago by Dick, mostly in matte blue, with high-polish blue on the side flats of the slide, the trigger, safety lever, and magazine catch. This combination of matte and high-polish is now often used by the manufacturers of new handguns, and is seen on both automatic pistols and revolvers. One practical advantage to this pattern is that the matte top prevents light reflections in the sighting plane. Among the military and police-type handguns in today's market, it is not unusual to see the entire gun in matte finish, with no polished areas.

The texture of the finish is entirely controlled by the pre-finish polishing—or lack of it. To produce the matte finish, the surface is blasted with fine sand or glass beads under high pressure. Another surface treatment, often seen on stainless steel guns, is the "brushed" finish. This is less dull than the matte surface, but is not as shiny as a high-polish. The brushed finish will show "lines" across the surface. This type of finish is not restricted to the stainless steel handguns. The barrel of my Star Model 28 pistol is blued, and its barrel in the ejection port area is finished this way.

There are times when routine refinishing of any type is definitely not advisable. When the handgun in question has substantial collector value, any ideas about refinishing should be considered very cautiously. In this area, I have seen some real atrocities. One that I particularly remember was a nickel-plated Luger, seen on a display table at a gun show. There were, by the way, *no* factory-nickeled Lugers. Two things made this one especially gruesome: It had obviously been in like-new condition before plating, as all corners were sharp and its markings were clear. And, it was a super-rare Krieghoff! The plating had instantly reduced it from a $1,000 collector piece to a $300 "shooter."

I have managed to prevent a few disasters of this sort. A fellow recently asked me to reblue a Walther P-38, and, as he put it, "get rid of that ugly gray finish, and replace those metal grips." When I told him that he was about to ruin a rare "Gray Ghost" Walther, and devalue it by about two-thirds, he was amazed. He wisely decided against refinishing, and later sold the Walther to a collector. The amount he received was enough to cover the cost of two fine new handguns.

When a valuable collector piece is in only slightly worn condition, with even half of the original finish left, it should be kept well-protected from rust and otherwise left alone. If it is

The author's 7.65mm Commerical Luger, having 90 percent of its original blue finish, is a good example of the type of handgun that should *not* be refinished.

This is not the Krieghoff mentioned in the text, but it is a good World War One Erfurt Luger. Or, it was, before its collector value was cancelled by a layer of nickel plate.

very worn, or has areas of pitting, a restoration might be considered. This goes far beyond a routine reblue or replating. It involves special methods that will restore the surfaces, as near as possible, to the original factory specifications. For older handguns, this often means having a restoration specialist use the slow-rust blue process, and restore the "straw" color or casehardening color to certain parts. In some cases, original markings are deepened by recutting. It's

much more expensive than regular refinishing, but definitely worth it.

Early nickel-plated revolvers are easier to restore to factory-original finish. First, the electrolytic process is used in reverse to strip the remains of the old plating from the main parts. Light polishing is done, to remove any small surface pitting, but the contours and markings are carefully preserved. The barrel, cylinder, frame, and screws are then re-nickeled. The

A badly pitted Smith & Wesson Model 1880 revolver before restoration. Note especially the areas on the barrel, and the crude homemade barrel latch screw, just above the cylinder.

Here is the same Smith & Wesson revolver, after its restoration by the author and Dick Floyd. Careful polishing before re-nickeling has eliminated the worst of the pits. A replacement was made for the barrel latch screw. The hammer and trigger were color-casehardened, and the barrel latch and trigger guard were blued.

hammer and trigger are color-casehardened, and the barrel latch and trigger guard are blued. This is a typical pattern, but of course there are variations with individual guns. When all of this is properly done, the gun will look almost exactly as it did when it originally left the factory.

Among collectors, there are two schools of thought in regard to restoration. The absolute purist considers any handgun that has been refinished, even by careful restoration, to be prac-

tically worthless as a collector piece. These collectors would rather have a gun in very worn condition, with only traces of the original finish remaining, than one that has been skillfully restored. The other group sees nothing wrong with restored pieces, as long as the work is done by an expert, with the result being as close as possible to the original factory finish.

I tend to agree, most of the time, with the latter group. Several years ago, I was graciously

Another restoration, a Smith & Wesson Model 1878, done along the same lines.

loaned a super-rare Adler pistol by a collector, one of two that I have seen. The Adler that I photographed for a magazine article was a fine restoration, blued by the slow rust method, with the appropriate small parts restored to straw color. The other Adler that I had seen was definitely factory original in all respects. I had the restored pistol overnight, disassembled it, and studied it thoroughly. I didn't know it was a restoration until I was later told by the owner!

Getting back to regular refinishing, there are other attractive uses of contrast in addition to the combination of matte and polished surfaces mentioned earlier. Some of these combinations even have practical aspects. I have a Webley Mark VI revolver that has been converted to fire 45 Auto Rim (or 45 Auto in clips), and some previous owner had the main parts expertly reblued. The hammer, trigger, cylinder retainer, retainer lever, and breech face piece had been

A British Webley Mark VI, converted to fire 45 Auto Rim, and nicely reblued by someone before the author obtained it. The hammer, trigger, cylinder retainer, and breech face piece are finished in bright nickel.

nickeled. From an appearance viewpoint, it was just enough to highlight the excellent blue. It was also practical, as the nickeled parts, especially the hammer, trigger, and breech face, are parts that are subject to wear from friction or handling.

A similar application of different finishes to certain parts is often used by manufacturers on new handguns. For many years, Smith & Wesson revolvers have had hammers and triggers that are surfaced in color-casehardening, a practice that enhances both appearance and wear properties. Several of the new double action automatic pistols have triggers or hammers, often both, that are surfaced in hard chrome. Color-casehardening is also used in automatics. My Star FM and Star BKM pistols have this finish

on the hammers. When you consider the friction of the slide on an auto pistol hammer, a harder surface is an obvious asset.

Let's look now at some of the finishes that are available, and their various properties. Some are more durable than others, and some are more resistant to certain elements that will quickly affect other finished surfaces. Several of the finishes that are very resistant to wear, rust, or corrosion are also unattractive, in the estimation of the traditionalist. So, in this respect, the choice of a finish may be a compromise. One observer, viewing a handgun in my office that has a new and very tough finish, commented that it looked like a "toy gun." On the other hand, this particular gun could be left out in the rain for a month, and it wouldn't rust.

Brown

It's now used principally on modern muzzle-loaders, and for restoring antique blackpowder handguns. Like blue, it is actually a controlled rusting process. It differs from blue in its chemical composition, and in its surface texture. Even

with a high pre-application polish, the surface will not be bright. Among the finishes that are discussed here, browning is unique in that it can be applied well without hot-bath immersion. The metal can be warmed, with a propane torch

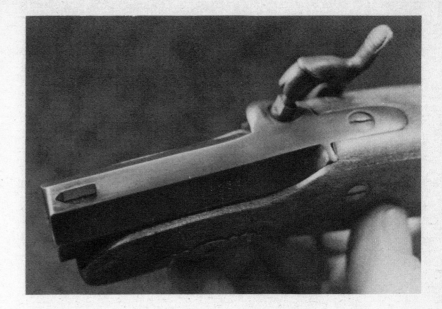

This percussion derringer, built from a kit, was finished in brown by Paul M. Fulkerson.

or in an oven, and the browning solution swabbed onto the surface.

My daughter's husband, Paul M. Fulkerson, has done quite a few modern muzzle-loaders in this way, and the rich brown finish is beautiful. Birchwood Casey makes a fine Plum Brown solution, and Dixie Gun Works, Union City, Tennessee 38261, also offers an excellent browning solution. Brownells has Rick Schrieber's Laurel Mountain Forge browning solution, used by many professional blackpowder gunsmiths. There is really no reason that browning couldn't be used on modern handguns, but there are two things against it. Its appearance would be a little strange, and there are more durable finishes available.

Blue

By a large margin, blue is the most popular and the most economical finish. A controlled oxidation of the steel surface, it varies in color from a very bluish light tone to a deep shade that is almost black. The color is the result of several factors, including the chemical composition of the bluing salts, the temperature of the bath, and the type of steel to which it is applied. A reddish tone is sometimes produced when the temperature of the bath is too high, when the steel is a heat-treated type, or when the steel is a very low-carbon casting. A good example of the latter would be the framed of some of the older lower-priced revolvers, some which were bare-

ly more than cast iron. Brownells has an additive called Oxynate S that prevents the red color when added to the bluing bath.

There are actually three methods of producing a blue finish. The hot bath method, using caustic salts, is the most often used, but there are other ways. There is a modern version of the Old Belgian Method, using Brownells Dicropan IM. This "hot water" bluing uses no caustic salts, and is slower, but it can produce a beautiful finish. The other method is the old "slow rust" process, as mentioned earlier in regard to restoration. It also is slow, but the results are worth the wait. Brownells has the Pilkington

Depending on the solution used, and other factors, the color of a hot-bath finish can range from a light blue to almost black, the latter illustrated by this Iver Johnson hammerless revolver. On a gun with a very dark finish, light-colored grips make a nice contrast.

Rust Blue solution for this method.

The traditionalist will always choose blue as a handgun finish, and its does have a handsome appearance. To many people, a pistol or revolver just doesn't look like a gun unless it's blued. It must be admitted, though, that blue does have some disadvantages. When it is subjected to continued rubbing, as in a holster, blue will wear off in time no matter how expertly it was applied. If the handgun is carried or kept in a humid atmosphere, or next to the body and in contact with perspiration, it will eventually rust.

Keeping the surface treated with a protectant oil will help, but it won't entirely prevent it.

From the standpoint of user choice, blue is better for sporting or target handguns, which would normally have lighter use, with less wear factor. For personal defense or law enforcement carrying, or other security applications, the constant wear and exposure to oxidizing or corrosive atmospheres would call for something more positively protective. In former times, before the advent of stainless steel handguns, the usual choice for this purpose was nickel plating.

Nickel

Like all other true plating, nickel plating is an electrolytic process. The part to be plated is suspended from a non-conducting rod in an electrolytic solution that contains the plating material in suspension. The part is connected to a negative electric terminal, or cathode, while a bar of pure nickel is suspended from a positive terminal, or anode. When the current is applied, the positive ions of nickel in the solution are deposited on the part, and are replaced in the

solution by nickel from the bar. The process is reversible, and is used in that way to strip worn and peeling nickel from a handgun that is to be re-plated. After this is done, the polishing and other preparations are the same as for rebluing.

Nickel has the advantage of being rust-proof, and it is resistant to perspiration and other corrosives. Its surface will tend to discolor in certain atmospheres and with age, but it can be re-polished to its original lustre. As long as the nickel

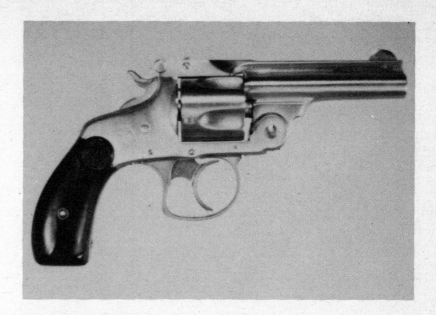

There was no attempt at restoration on this Smith & Wesson Model 1880 revolver. Its owner wanted it only for practical use, and it was finished entirely in satin nickel. Though not to factory original pattern, it's attractive, and well-protected.

An unusual treatment of a Browning Model 1922 pistol. Custom grips were made of sheet brass, and the entire gun, including the grips, was finished in bright nickel. The grips were extended at upper rear to cover the opening for the manual safety, which was missing. The result was a very flat and easily concealable piece.

surface remains intact, it is an excellent protection for the steel it covers. It also wears well, having greater thickness and resistance to abrasion than blue. As with other finishes, nickel can be done in a polished or matte style, according to the preparation of the surface of the steel. It is possible to nickel plate some aluminum alloy parts, but certain alloy combinations react to the acids in the electrolytic bath, and can be damaged.

If use of the handgun includes personal protection or law enforcement, there is one disadvantage in a nickel finish: Its bright surface is light-reflective, and in a serious situation it could betray your location to an adversary, even in darkness. On the other hand, I once knew a law officer who carried a factory-nickeled Smith & Wesson Model 29, and when asked about it he commented that when it became necessary to get out the gun, he wanted the miscreants to

Before the application of satin nickel, the barrel of this Iver Johnson revolver was shortened, and it was left sightless for pocket use. The satin finish here is the "brushed" type, looking a lot like stainless steel.

know that the encounter had turned serious. In sporting use, in the daylight, light reflection from a polished nickel finish could startle game, and it could also interfere with sighting. Even if the top of the handgun is in matte texture, the sights would be less clear in bright sunlight. For this reason, many factory-nickeled handguns have sights of blued steel.

Another disadvantage of nickel is one that occurs only with age and long wear. If there is sufficient wear at any sharp edge, the nickel will often start to peel. Eventually, areas of bare steel will be exposed, and rust will follow. The problem of peeling can also be accelerated by the heat and high pressures of normal use in revolvers, especially the magnums. The areas af-

fected are the front face of the cylinder and the adjoining areas on the front of the frame. It's not unusual to find an otherwise perfect nickel finish with some erosion in these areas, if a lot of shooting is done.

As a practical finish, nickel has largely been superseded by several finishes that are more durable and less reflective. In recent years, my only use of it has been in the restoration of handguns that originally had this finish, and for plating certain small parts as an accent on blued guns, as on the Welbey revolver described earlier. It has some value in these uses, but as an over-all finish for working handguns, it's my feeling that its time is past.

Chrome

Chrome, as a metallic substance, was discovered in 1797. For more than a hundred years, it was little more than a laboratory curiosity. Because of its high resistance to heat and chemicals, the old methods of extracting it from chromium ore made it difficult and expensive to

obtain. By around 1915 new extraction methods had been developed, and chrome began to be a valued additive to steel alloys. Along the way, it also began to be used in protective plating on many items, including handguns.

In several ways, chrome plating as a protec-

Two of the chromed pistols mentioned in the text, a Beretta Model 948 and a Savage Model 1908. Both were done in a combination of matte and high polish chrome.

tive finish for handguns is superior to nickel. Its surface is much harder, more resistant to scratches. It is resistant to chemicals that can mar nickel, and it is not subject to the slight tarnishing effect that can occur with nickel in some atmospheres. The hard surface of chrome also resists wear better, and this is less likely to expose bare steel after long and tough usage. In appearance, it is whiter than nickel, and its matching to polished alloy has already been noted.

Chrome is, I am told, more difficult to apply properly than nickel, and this may explain, in part, its relatively rare use as a new-gun finish by manufacturers. Two Spanish gunmakers, Star and Astra, still offer it as a finish option, and there are a few others. As a practical finish, chrome shares one drawback with nickel—it is highly light-reflective. Also, like nickel, it can begin to peel if its surface integrity is broken. In this respect it is somewhat more brittle than nickel, and will tend to flake away in larger pieces. I think of it in the same way as nickel—it's a good protective finish, but better ones have been developed.

Black Chrome

Ten years ago, anyone who owned a stainless steel handgun and wanted it to have a dark finish had only one real option—black chrome. As far as I know, this finish was offered by only one firm, the Marker Machine Company of Charleston, Illinois. I don't know whether the Marker company is still in business, but I do know that by the late 70s they were no longer offering black chrome as a firearm finish. Black Chrome was a mixture of a black oxide and regular chrome, and was applied in the same way as other plating. Only Mr. Marker knew the exact proportions of the mixture, and to my knowledge no other firm has since offered this finish.

Back when black chrome was available, I sent two Browning HP pistols to Marker, and had one done in high-polish black chrome, the

A Browning Hi-Power, finished in matte black chrome by Marker Machine Company. The hammer was done in hard chrome.

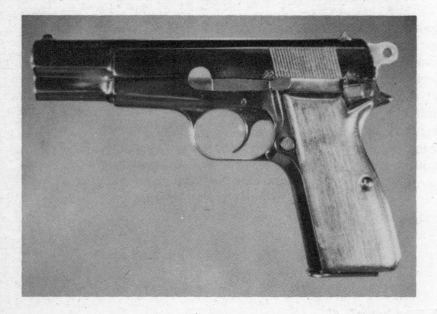

Another example of Marker black chrome, this one done in high polish.

other in matte finish. The matte-style black chrome was an even grey, looking very much like a smooth Parkerizing. The bright finish was much more attractive, having a deep black lustre that reminded me of the blue on early British commercial revolvers. The high-polish gun belonged to a friend who later moved to the West Coast, so I don't know how that finish has held up. My own wartime HP had the satin finish, and it has since been refinished, in Armoloy.

Because of the oxide in the mixture, black chrome was a little softer than regular chrome, and was more susceptible to scratches and wear. Even so, it offered better protection than blue, as it was actually a coating, rather than a change in the surface. And, for a while, it was "the" way to apply a dark finish on stainless steel handguns.

Silver and Gold

Except for occasional use on presentation pieces, the high-value metals are not usually chosen for finishing entire handguns. Adolf Hitler once owned a richly-engraved Walther pistol that was entirely gold-plated. I once examined an Astra Model 300 that was owned by Hermann Goering, also engraved, and it was silver plated. Quite a while back, I had Dick Floyd do a 25 Galesi pistol entirely in gold, with the small parts in nickel. This was done at the request of a fellow who was giving the pistol to his girlfriend. It was rather . . . ah . . . gaudy.

In practical use, silver and gold are best used as a decorative finish for small parts, such as triggers and safety levers, on handguns that are mostly showpieces. These metals are also used to fill engraved lines or highlight figures on elaborately decorated commemorative pieces. Both metals are really too soft to use as a total finish, and silver will inevitably tarnish unless it is frequently polished. Also, especially in the case of gold, the expense of having a large handgun plated would be prohibitive for the average owner.

Parkerizing

True Parkerizing was developed by the Parker Company of Detroit, Michigan, around 1925. There are actually quite a few different phosphate-finish processes, each producing a slightly different tone or color. On our military arms, U.S. Ordnance has used three principal types. The one most used, manganese iron, gives a dark grey to black finish that is the most wear-resistant. Zinc phosphate produces a light grey shade and this is the finish that was used on many World War Two guns. Duracoat is a phosphate coating over zinc plating, and this is the one that gives a greenish (olive drab) appearance. Zinc phosphate and Duracoat have not been used by the U.S. military for many years.

In comercial use, these processes also have various trade names. The manganese iron is called by the Parker company Lubrite #2. For the same finish, the Heatbath Corporation of Springfield, Massachusetts, uses the designation M-22. The application of Parkerizing, by whatever name, is similar to bluing, but special tanks of 300-series stainless steel are required. The temperatures involved are important, much lower, and keeping the heating even is critical. The preferred heat source is electricity. U.S. Ordnance specifications require grit-blasting with fine silica sand before phosphating.

About ten years ago, I had a well-worn and mismatched Chicom Type 54 pistol (a Chinese copy of the Russian Tokarev) re-phosphated by the manganese iron method. The finish was an even dark grey, and the smaller rust pits that were present were eliminated by the pretreatment sand-blasting. I still have this pistol, and the finish has held up well over the years. The firm that did it for me is no longer in business, and the only company that I know of that routinely offers Parkerizing is Electrofilm, Incorporated, 27727 Avenue Scott, Valencia, California 91355. For the gunsmiths reading this who would like to try it, Brownells has Amer-Lene, which when used properly will give a nice grey phosphate finish.

Photographed before refinishing, this Chicom Type 54 pistol had almost none of its original finish left, and there were areas of pitting.

Parkerizing eliminated most of the pitting, and gave the Type 54 an almost new look.

Color-Casehardening

Ordinary casehardening of steel surfaces is a heat-and-quench process that involves slow heating of the item to a certain temperature which is maintained for a period of time, then plunging the item into water or some other liquid, depending on the type of steel. This treatment imparts a very hard surface that is resistant to rust. However, this treatment will not neces-

Right—When a custom gun-smith and an expert refinisher decide to see how pretty they can make a rough kit gun, the results are sometimes surprising. After all of the meetings of the external parts were trued and polished, the barrel, wedge, cylinder and screws were blued. The grip frame parts were bright nickeled, and the frame and other parts were color-casehardened. It's a beautiful handgun.

Left—This kit gun from Dixie Gun Works was mechanically fitted, but externally, only the cylinder was smooth.

Right—A closer view of the color-casehardening. While this gun is a modern black-powder copy, this finish is often used in the restoration of older pieces.

sarily produce the attractive mottling, the "oil-slick" colors, that constitute color-casehardening. There are several ways to achieve this, and all involve the use of various chemicals in conjunction with the heat and quenching. Some of the chemicals used for this purpose in earlier times were poisonous.

I'm not sure how Dick Floyd obtains his beautiful color-casehardening effects—as with many practitioners it's his own secret. I have had some success in producing a similar cosmetic effect by swabbing the surface with cold blue in a random pattern before heat-treatment. It might be noted here that the straw coloring of small parts is also done by the heat-and-quench method, but without chemicals. Here, the temperature is all-important, and it takes an expert's eye and familiarity with the steel to get it right. In the restoration of older handguns, color-casehardening and "strawing" are often important.

Anodizing

In a process that is similar to electro-plating, but with different materials, aluminum alloy is color-coated by a method called anodizing. To harmonize with the finish of blued steel parts, most of the anodizing used on handguns is a black or blue-black color. Actually, any color is possible. A few years back, a few snub-nosed versions of the Hi-Standard 22 Sentinel, aimed for the ladies' market, were anodized in turquoise blue and (ugh!) *pink!* Yes, they looked just as awful as you're imagining them.

In wear resistance, anodizing is on about the same level as nickel plating. However, because of the relative softness of the aluminum alloy that it covers, it is more susceptible to scratches and other damage. When the anodized frame of a handgun begins to lose its finish, or is scratched, it's possible to mask very small bright spots by using a permanent-ink felt-tipped marker. When the steel parts of the handgun are being reblued, and the entire alloy frame needs refinishing, there's a problem, because gun shops do not normally have the expensive equipment for re-anodizing. Few facilities, outside of the gun factory, do anodizing on a single-piece basis. There is one that I know of: Techplate Engineering, 1571-H South Sunkist, Anaheim, Californa 92806.

I have often seen attempts by owners to re-do a badly scratched or worn frame by using black spray-enamel, but the ordinary hardware-store type will not adhere well to the alloy, and it soon flakes off. Brownells has an "Aluma-Hyde" kit that is the next best thing to genuine re-anodizing. It consists of a zinc-chromate primer and a special nitro-cellulose lacquer, and while they make no claim that it's as good as anodizing, it looks good and wears well. Of course, if the handgun is being done in any sort of plating, it's best to just finish the alloy to match the texture of the other surfaces, and leave it bare, as was done on the Beretta 22 described earlier.

Teflon-S

Let's say at the start that Teflon is a registered trademark of the DuPont company, in whose laboratories the process was discovered. In firearms applications, the principal purveyor is West Coast SECOA, 3915 Highway 98 South, Lakeland, Florida 33801. In the first years following its discovery, Teflon was used mostly on household utensils such as frying pans and steam irons. Then, someone realized that this space-age coating would also be a fine protective finish for firearms. Since its beginning, Teflon has undergone several improvements, and these were noted by added designations—Teflon II, for example. The tough industrial process presently used by SECOA is called Teflon-S.

Teflon-S is not the same as the Teflon used on kitchen utensils. It's an industrial variation that is cured at 650 degrees to form three layers, the bottom strata forming a chemical bond with the surface of the metal. All parts can be coated except the springs and the bore, and Teflon-S has a low friction coefficient, smoothing the action. It also sheds water and powder residues, is self-lubricating, and is non-reflective. When

A 25 Raven (above) and a 22 Jennings (below), both with Teflon-S finish in black. These were the first pistols to offer the Teflon finish as a factory option. It has many advantages.

properly applied, by a DuPont-licensed firm like SECOA, it is very durable. It is resistant to nitro solvents, and it is unaffected by fingerprints, perspiration, and salt water.

If Teflon-S has any disadvantage, it would be that its surface can be scratched by contact with any sharp object. However, it is not "soft," and with reasonable care it will last a long time. It is particularly popular as a handgun finish among law enforcement people in coastal locations, where the guns used are in constant exposure to salt air. It is also a good choice as a finish for handguns that are kept or used on boats.

Armoloy and Other Hard Chromes

Armoloy was the first of several hard chrome applications to firearms. Even harder than most industrial chromes, it has a Rockwell C number of about 70, which means that it's harder than a good file. Describing this finish as "durable" would be an understatement. Of course, it is also impervious to rust and corrosion. It will even survive temperatures up to 1300 degrees.

A nearly-new Turkish MKE pistol, shown before it was readied for Armoloy finish. The original finish was a good blue.

The MKE pistol, shown detail-stripped. Everything but the springs, ready to be sent to Armoloy.

The same group of MKE parts, shown after the Armoloy finish was applied, before reassembly.

The MKE in Armoloy, with a new pair of Sile walnut grip panels. In addition to enhanced appearance and protection, the trigger pull was smoother.

An Armoloy-surfaced handgun might even survive a fire and need only replacement of the springs and grips. Strangely, though, the application is a low-temperature process, only 136 degrees Fahrenheit.

Armoloy has a thickness of only two tenthousandths of an inch, so there is no reassembly problem after the finish is applied. Its appearance is an attractive silver-grey, with a matte texture that is actually less light-reflective than blue. A nice side-effect is a marked reduction in friction. Steel-on-steel has a friction coefficient of 0.20, and when two surfaces are coated in Armoloy, this is reduced to 0.12. Once, as a test-piece, I had Armoloy applied to a 380 MKE pistol, the Turkish copy of the Walther PP. After Armoloy, the double action trigger pull was markedly smoother and lighter. My Browning HP also has an Armoloy finish. The Armoloy company is at 204 East Daggett

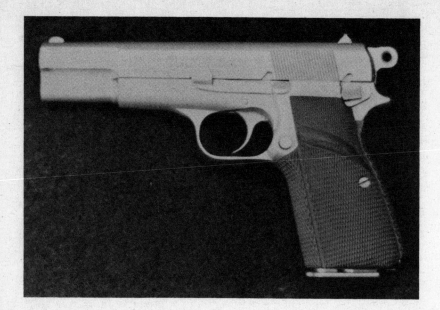

The author's Browning HP, shown earlier in matte black chrome, with its present Armoloy finish, applied in 1974. This photo was made in 1984.

Street, Fort Worth, Texas 76104.

The other hard chrome finishes have virtually identical properties, including a Rockwell C number of around 70 and all of the advantages noted above. There are slight appearance differences, in texture and in color, though all are basically silver-grey. One of the other hard chrome finishes is Metalife (Box 53, Reno Industrial Park, Reno, Pennsylvania 16343). I have examined a handgun with Metalife finish, but I haven't actually given it a carrying and use test. From all reports, though, it's excellent. Another hard chrome finish, and one that I have used, is Metaloy (Route 3, Box 211-D, Berryville, Arkansas 72616).

Metaloy is a darker grey than Armoloy, and seems to have a smoother surface texture. That factor is, of course, partially controlled by the pre-application preparation of the steel. Still, the Metaloy surface, compared to the Armoloy on my Browning HP, seemed "slicker." All of these hard chrome finishes are practically immune to scratches, but if they are hit or scraped with an object that is hard enough and sharp enough, they can be marked. It will be just that —a bright mark, with the actual surface unbroken. If this happens, a little careful rubbing with a mild abrasive of the right grade can restore the original look. For durability and protection, the hard chromes are the ultimate finish.

Electroless Nickel

As its name implies, electroless nickel is a nickel-based surfacing that is applied without an electric current. The process was discovered around 1945, and in recent years it has seen increasing use on firearms. It has several advantages over regular electrolytic nickel plating, the most important being an absolutely uniform thickness over the entire part. With regular nickel, the edges receive the largest deposit of nickel, the flat surfaces a thinner plate, and recesses often get no plating at all. Also, the chemicals used for regular plating are usually forms of metallic cyanide salts, adding expense to the shipping and the cost of the finish. While electroless

Someone, apparently an amateur, had attempted to apply electroless nickel to this Match Target Colt. It turned out very badly.

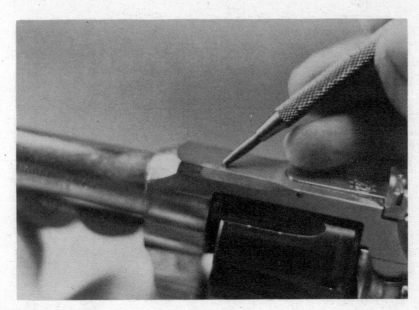

The tool is pointing to one of several areas on the Colt where there were obvious flaws in the finish.

nickel does use acids in the process, these are routinely shippable or can be purchased locally.

Electroless nickel uses heat bath tanks with mild agitation, and maintaining certain temperatures is a critical point. This finish can be used on regular steel, stainless steel, nickel alloys, beryllium copper, sintered metals, and aluminum alloys. It can't be used on zinc alloys. Its Rockwell C number ranges from 49 to 53, and it will pass a 180-degree bending test without cracking or peeling. Parts finished in electroless nickel will withstand at least 96 hours of direct salt spray without rusting. Its external appearance can be either "frosted" or polished, or a combination of these. Since it's not plain pure nickel, but a special alloy, it is whiter than regular nickel plating, and can be done to look very much like stainless steel.

It's an excellent finish. Brownells has all of the components to do electroless nickel finish,

The Colt was expertly refinished in Metaloy. Note the same area, indicated by the tool.

Left and below—Two views of the Match Target Colt with Metaloy finish. This time, it was done *right*.

and while their address appears elsewhere in this book, I'll repeat it here: Brownells, Incorporated, Route Two, Box One, Montezuma, Iowa 50171. In the words of master gunsmith Ralph Walker, who wrote the EN instruction book for Brownells, "The equipment needed is minimal —a couple of plastic pans, an old sink, a heat source, a couple of Grandma's blue-rock canners, and a stirring mechanism. Plus, the patience and intelligence to read and follow the

Above and below—Two examples of Nitex, one of the best-known commerical forms of electroless nickel. In some applications, it's difficult to distinguish it from stainless steel.

instructions, particularly the cleaning instructions, to the letter.''

One of the best-known commercial electroless nickel finishes is Nitex. A few years ago, at the SHOT Show, I examined a Colt Python that I would have sworn was made of stainless steel—but at that time, the Python was not offered in stainless. It was Nitex-finished, of course. Ed House and his people do a fine job. Nitex, Incorporated, is located at 2910 Belmeade in Carrollton, Texas 75006. The phone number is 214-446-1197. At the moment, the only gun that I have with an electroless nickel finish is my Bushmaster pistol. I've given it some fairly hard usage over the past year, and so far the surface still looks fine.

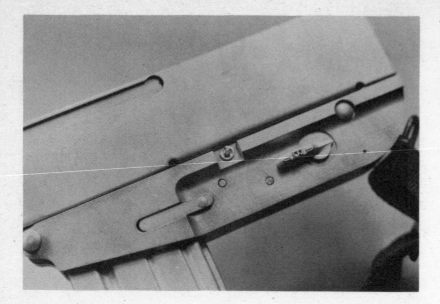

A current-production Bushmaster pistol, finished by the factory in electroless nickel. This relatively new finish has many advantages.

Lubri-Bond

Surface finishes of this type are both a finish and a lubricant. One that I have tried is Lubri-Bond, a process offered by Electrofilm, Incorporated, 27727 Avenue Scott, Valencia, California 91355. Lubri-Bond is principally molybdenum disulfide in a resin base, and it can reduce the friction between mating parts to a figure as low as 0.02. The steel to which Lubri-

An early factory application of a lubricant finish was on this now-discontinued Plainfeld model 71 pistol.

As a test piece in the Electrofilm labs, this Colt Commando Special was finished in Lubri-Bond, *except* for the hammer, cylinder and sideplate, then subjected to salt-fog testing. You can see the results in the lower photo.

Bond is applied should be sand-blasted or glass-beaded, and ideally, it should also be Parkerized. In factory application, Type M military phosphate is used, then the Lubri-Bond is cured by air-drying for 18 to 24 hours, or heat-treated at 300 degrees for 1 hour.

With this application, and using air-drying, it's even possible to do the springs along with all of the other internal parts. The resulting finish is a light grey color with a smooth matte surface. It can be scratched, and there will be bright silver marks where parts engage, but this doesn't mean the finish has been penetrated. Molybdenum disulfide has a silver color when compressed, and its properties are not lost. Since the finish is actually a high-grade lubricant, there's really no need to use any oil. I had Lubri-Bond applied by Electrofilm to a well-worn Smith & Wesson Model 1905 and without any added lubricant its action is very smooth.

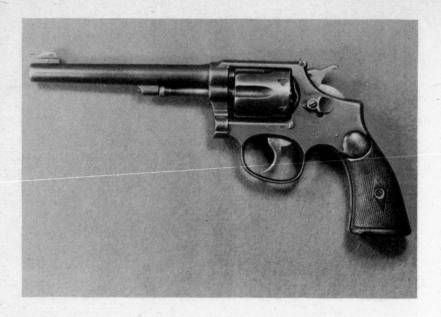

Two views of a venerable and well-worn Smith & Wesson Model 1905, before refinishing. All of the original blue was gone, and it had a patina of surface rust.

Externally, there is also no need for the addition of any protectants. Lubri-Bond meets or exceeds the various military specifications for corrosion resistance, and will withstand 240 hours of salt-fog exposure without rusting. This is the equivalent of immersing the gun in salt water for more than 6 months. The surface is dry, and dirt or sand will not stick to it. For matching, it can be applied to aluminum alloys. It can also be applied to stainless steel, and will not only dark-en the surface, but will also prevent the galling that is a problem with some early handguns made of this material.

In addition to factory-applied Lubri-Bond, Electrofilm also offers a kit for those who want to apply it themselves. It contains two 3-ounce aerosol containers, one a de-greaser and the other Lubri-Bond. The retail price of the kit is about $10. When the finish is applied by Electrofilm, the cost is comparable to the average

The same Model 1905 Smith & Wesson, after Lubri-Bond was applied. All of the internal parts and springs were also done—everything but the blade of the front sight, which was nickel silver, and was intentionally omitted.

reblue job. A few years ago, the now-discontinued Plainfield Model 17 pistol came with a factory-applied lubricant finish. I have one of these guns, and the finish is the same as when the pistol was new.

Kolene QPQ

The cryptic letters above stand for "Quench-Polish-Quench," and they constitute a registered trademark of Kolene Corporation, 12890 Westwood, Detroit, Michigan 48223. While this finish can be used as a superb corrosion-resistant surfacing for regular steel (it outperforms both hard chrome and electroless nickel), one of its most interesting qualities is that it can give stainless steel a fine, deep black finish that is extremely durable. My first encounter with the

tractive finish is a salt-bath liquid-nitriding, followed by mechanical polishing, then a final immersion in the quench bath. This sequence creates a unique metallurgical surface. The oxygen-rich epsilon iron nitride on the surface has corrosion resistance and wear resistance properties that surpass chrome and nickel. At this time, the QPQ finish is available only on the Fraser pistol, but the corporation is licensing its process to some commercial heat-treating companies, and

The Fraser 25 Automatic pistol, factory-finished in Kolene QPQ black. Under its black finish, the little gun is stainless steel.

Kolene QPQ finish was its use on the little Fraser 25 Automatic pistol. Made by the company that produced the stainless steel Bauer pistol, the Fraser is the same gun with a different name.

My own Fraser 25 with the QPQ black finish has been carried and fired with some frequency for about 7 months now, and the finish still looks like the day it was taken out of the factory box. The process that makes this tough and at-

one of them is sure to offer it as a general firearms finish.

There is another black finish for stainless steel, called SS Satin Black, offered by Clinton River Gun Service, 30016 South River Road, Mount Clemens, Michigan 48045. I have not seen an example of this, and have very little data on it. According to a company spokesman, it is a hot-bath process, and does not involve any plating. For those who want to inquire about

The frame of the Steyr GB pistol has an unusual (for firearms) black "crackle" finish. It seems to be very durable.

Here are examples of SS Satin Black, applied to the stainless steel Ruger Security Six and Redhawk.

this new finish by phone, the number is 313-468-1090.

There are a few odd finishes that I haven't detailed here because their use as replacement finishes would seem to be doubtful. Prior to World War Two, French military handguns were finsihed in a black baked-on enamel that was fairly durable, considering the way it withstood hard usage. Similar "paint" finishes have been used occasionally by others. More re-cently, a black "crackle" finish is being used on the frame of the superb Steyr GB pistol. I don't know whether it's a baked enamel or is otherwise applied, but I do know that it's very tough. I cut through it in polishing the feed ramp on the frame, but it wasn't easy.

In selecting one of the finishes described here for a particular handgun, there are three main factors to be considered: Appearance, Protection, and Light Reflection, not necessarily in

French military handguns of an earlier time were finished in a black baked-on enamel. On this Model 1892 revolver it is beginning to wear off, but considering the hard usage, it was remarkably tough.

that order. One of these factors will be of more importance in a particular application than the other two, and the finish can be chosen on that basis. With those points in mind, the decision shouldn't be difficult.